Native Sons

*Philadelphia Baseball Players Who
Made the Major Leagues*

OTHER BOOKS BY RICH WESTCOTT

The Phillies Encyclopedia
(with Frank Bilovsky)

Diamond Greats

The New Phillies Encyclopedia
(with Frank Bilovsky)

Phillies '93: An Incredible Season

Philadelphia's Old Ballparks

Mike Schmidt

Masters of the Diamond

No-Hitters: The 225 Games, 1893–1999
(with Allen Lewis)

Splendor on the Diamond

Great Home Runs of the 20th Century

A Century of Philadelphia Sports

Winningest Pitchers: Baseball's 300-Game Winners

Tales from the Phillies Dugout

NATIVE SONS

*Philadelphia Baseball Players Who
Made the Major Leagues*

Rich Westcott

FOREWORD BY BILL CAMPBELL

TEMPLE UNIVERSITY PRESS *Philadelphia*

Temple University Press, Philadelphia 19122
Copyright © 2003 by Rich Westcott
All rights reserved
Published 2003
Printed in the United States of America

⊗ The paper used in this publication meets the requirements of
the American National Standard for Information Sciences—Permanence
of Paper for Printed Library Materials, ANSI Z39.48-1984

Library of Congress Cataloging-in-Publication Data

Westcott, Rich.
   Native sons : Philadelphia baseball players who made the major leagues /
   Rich Westcott ; foreword by Bill Campbell.
      p.   cm.
   Includes bibliographical references.
   ISBN 1-59213-215-4 (pbk. : alk. paper)
      1. Baseball players—Pennsylvania—Philadelphia—Biography.   2. Baseball—
   Pennsylvania—Philadelphia—History.   I. Title.

GV865.A1W448 2003
796.357′092′074811—dc21
   [B]

2003050793

2 4 6 8 9 7 5 3 1

To Lois

My rock, my beacon, my lifelong MVP,

whose support, generosity, kindness, encouragement,

and enthusiasm know no boundaries;

and

To Chris, Susan, Lora, and Amy

Our four exemplary offspring, whose triumphant journeys

through life provide an unending source of

joy and pride.

Contents

Foreword

In *Native Sons,* Rich Westcott has written about all the local guys who can trace their baseball origins to the Philadelphia area. I can trace my own origins to the same place, which is probably why he asked me to write this foreword.

Most of these guys made it in one fashion or another. Here I am pushing 80 and still struggling to make it. But I have one happy qualification. I have enjoyed an enviable seat in the broadcasting booth, describing the joys and sorrows, the successes and failures of many of these competitors. It is a seat I occupied with much pride and one that I vacated reluctantly.

I have been asked many times to describe the makeup of a typical Philadelphia baseball fan. I can only tell you about how I became one.

A baseball writer from the old *Evening Bulletin* named John Nolan lived next door to my family when I was a mere child. Mr. and Mrs. Nolan had no children, and my father was a baseball fan of the highest order. He and Mr. Nolan spent a lot of time at Shibe Park, and I gloried in listening to their tales of Jimmie Foxx and Lefty Grove and Jimmy Dykes and Al Simmons, and, of course, Connie Mack.

One October day in 1929 they took me to my first big league game. I was six years old—and going to a World Series game, yet! The Athletics versus the Chicago Cubs.

The A's, trailing, 8–0, going into the bottom of the seventh inning, scored 10 runs in that inning—something no team had done before or has done since. On that October day, at the age of six, I made a big decision about what I wanted to do with my life. And I've been doing it ever since. How could anyone ever wish to do anything else?

But even my longevity in the area has failed to prevent me from being constantly surprised by some of the things that Rich writes about in this book. Every successful book has to contain some surprises, and *Native Sons* is full of them.

First of all, I would never have believed that at least 350 Philadelphia-area players have reached the majors since 1900, or that many were among the greats of the game, including four Hall of Fame players, two Hall of Fame managers, four Most Valuable Players—one a three-time MVP—two four-time home run champions, and a three-time 20-game winner.

Remember Cal Abrams of the Brooklyn Dodgers, the guy Richie Ashburn threw out at home plate on the last day of the 1950 season to save the pennant for the Phillies? Did you know that Abrams was a local guy—a Philadelphia native? Maybe I knew that in 1950—I was at Ebbets Field when it happened—but I had forgotten his origin.

Because *Native Sons* brings back a lot of memories, it's great fun to read. It will remind you that "our guys" played the game with great effort, with much dignity, and with true affection. All the superb research and the solid writing make this book very special. You don't even have to be from Philadelphia to enjoy it.

Reggie Jackson received much of his publicity as "Mr. October" with the New York Yankees, but he came from Wyncote. Roy Campanella of the Brooklyn Dodgers, Mike Piazza of the New York Mets, Mickey Vernon of the Washington Senators, and Tom Lasorda, Danny Murtaugh, and Joe McCarthy, who won 15 pennants and 11 World Series among them, all swung the bat and threw the ball for the first time somewhere around your neighborhood or mine.

This book will also inspire some Hall of Fame controversy, which is never a bad idea. I hope that some of the electors get to read it because I think that at least two of our local guys have been shortchanged—namely, Mickey Vernon from Marcus Hook and Del Ennis from Olney.

Mickey played his entire career in other places, while Del was here with the Phillies for almost his entire time. Vernon played for 20 years, won two American League batting titles—beating out Ted Williams for one of them—collected 2,495 hits, and was one of the most picturesque first baseman who ever played the game. Ennis was the National League Rookie of the Year in 1946 when he hit .313 with 17 home runs. He knocked in 126 runs and had 31 homers when the Phillies won their first pennant in 35 years in 1950. And for almost a decade, Del carried the Phillies on his broad back offensively to the tune of some horribly misguided booing. He was a three-time All-Star, and, like Vernon, deserves more Hall of Fame consideration than he has received.

For historical reasons, the year 1863 has always stood out for me for an event never connected with baseball. That year, Abraham Lincoln gave his famous address at Gettysburg, which is not all that far from Philadelphia. But it wasn't until I read *Native Sons* that I realized that a team called the Athletics signed baseball's first professional player in that same year. He was a lefthanded second baseman, yet (how many of those have you seen?), who later became a sporting goods tycoon, and still later wound up as the first owner of the Phillies—without the concerns of revenue sharing, a payroll tax, a minimum wage, a disabled list, and discussions of drug testing at league meetings. (Of course, there was no formal league then.)

But having a lefthanded second baseman as an original owner could account for a lot of the Phillies' problems over the years. I have no doubt, however, that Rich Westcott will dig up a lefthanded second baseman somewhere who will be the subject of his next book.

If it turns out to be as good a read as *Native Sons,* it will be worth the wait.

Bill Campbell

NATIVE SONS

*Philadelphia Baseball Players Who
Made the Major Leagues*

Introduction

The Philadelphia area is the birthplace of the United States flag as well as America's first modern bank, theater, public school, zoo, electronic computer, locomotive, volunteer fire company, farmers' market, trade union, magazine, stock exchange, and professional surgery. It is the home of the Declaration of Independence, the Philadelphia Orchestra, the Philadelphia Museum of Art, Fairmount Park, and the Mummers Parade. Soft pretzels, cheese steaks, scrapple, and carbonated water originated in the region. Andrew Wyeth, Bill Cosby, Louisa May Alcott, Mario Lanza, Stephen Decatur, John Bartram, Will Smith, Ethel Barrymore, George McClellan, Thomas Eakins, Grace Kelly, W. C. Fields, Kim Delaney, and Benjamin Rush were all born in the area.

So, too, were a considerable number of major league baseball players.

When it comes to baseball, the phrase "local boy makes good" is one that has a special meaning in the Philadelphia area. Throughout the history of the game, the region has supplied players of every stripe to major league diamonds, in the process stamping itself as one of the nation's major reservoirs of baseball talent.

The region, of course, has no corner on the market. All big cities and their surrounding environs have made contributions to the national pastime. The Philadelphia metropolitan area has just done it bigger and better than most.

During the 20th century and into the 21st century, the number of the Philadelphia area's homegrown major leaguers has reached some 350. The list is restricted to players born—not just raised—in Philadelphia, the four surrounding counties (Bucks, Chester, Delaware, and Montgomery), the nearby counties of South Jersey (Burlington, Camden, Gloucester, and Salem), and New Castle County in northern Delaware. And that figure doesn't include pre-20th-century players, the many Negro League players from the area who were denied the chance to play major league baseball, or the large group of local minor leaguers who never made it to the top.

Of those who did make it to the majors, including 188 Philadelphians, some stayed for only a short time. Others spent many years in the big leagues. Some were good hitters, some were good fielders, some were good pitchers. And some were just plain good for nothing.

Many ranked among the greats of the game. The Philadelphia area can take pride as being the home of four Hall of Fame players and two Hall of Fame managers. The region has produced four Most Valuable Players, including one three-time winner. Two four-time home run kings come from the area. So do a two-time batting champion, a one-time batting leader, five league RBI leaders, and a three-time 20-game winner.

Philadelphia-area natives also were connected with many significant events in baseball. In World Series. In All-Star Games. In pennant clinchers. Three players from the region pitched no-hitters. Another player made an unassisted triple play. Several had connections with all-time records. And who would've thought that localites played key roles in the 1919 Black Sox scandal?

And this is just the tip of the iceberg. Numerous players compiled average statistical records but were integral components of their teams. More than a few played major roles on pennant-winning clubs. Many of them excelled in performing the finer points of the game.

The list of the region's big leaguers includes brothers, sons of big leaguers, and other relatives. There are multiple graduates of the same high school or college, notables in basketball, and players related to notables in other sports. The list includes players who most of us would have no idea were natives of the area. It also includes players who were born in the region and soon thereafter moved to another area.

The operative word here is "born." If a player was born in the Philadelphia area, he qualifies as a native and hence is listed in this book, even if he was raised elsewhere. (In a number of cases, players were born in hospitals in communities close to but not necessarily the same as the ones in which they grew up.) Conversely, several notable players grew up in the Philadelphia area but were born some other place. Thus they are not regarded as natives and are not featured in this volume.

The players to whom we do make claim, however, form an imposing list. There are Reggie Jackson and Goose Goslin. Herb Pennock and Bucky Walters. Roy Campanella and Del Ennis. Mickey Vernon and Eddie Stanky. Mike Piazza and Mike Scioscia. Bobby Shantz and Jamie Moyer, Jimmy Dykes and Harry Davis, Ray Narleski and Eddie Miksis. And among the region's 17 managers are skippers such as Tom Lasorda, Danny Murtaugh, and Joe McCarthy, who combined to win 15 pennants and 11 World Series.

Did you know that Cal Abrams came from the Philadelphia area? So did Buck Weaver. And Walt Masterson, Bill Dietrich, Jon Matlack, and Mark Gubicza, as well as Joe McEwing and Joe Kerrigan. There was also Sig Jakucki and Brook Jacoby. Socks Seibold and Rick Schu. Highball Wilson and Jack Daniels. Steve Frey and Joe Burns. Curtis King and John Knight. Harry Pearce and Bud Sharpe. Wid Conroy and Kid Gleason. And Pat Kelly and Pat Kelly.

Over the years, these people and many more have given major league baseball a decidedly Philadelphia flavor. Obviously, that flavor has been strongest on Philadelphia's own teams—the Phillies and the long-departed Athletics. But it extends virtually to all teams, each one in some way or another having been touched by native sons of the Philadelphia region. In fact, no less than 22 players from the region appeared in the major leagues during the 2001, 2002, or 2003 seasons.

So *Native Sons* is a book that celebrates the legions of local boys who reached the pinnacle of athletic achievement—the level to which all decent players aspire—by making good as major league baseball players. The group gives the area that made so many other significant contributions to the nation another special reason to be proud.

①

I would like to extend a special thanks to my friend Bill Campbell for writing the foreword for *Native Sons*. In the world of broadcasting, Bill, also a native son, is one of the all-time greats. He has been a fixture on local radio and television for more than 50 years, making him the dean of Philadelphia-area broadcasters. Over the years, Bill's majestic voice has been heard calling the games of the Phillies, Eagles, 76ers, and many more teams in the area. It is a special honor to me that he has written this foreword. I also want to express my gratitude to Doug Frambes, Sam Carchidi, Bob Bloss, and Jack Scheuer for their help in compiling information for this book.

1

Philly's Finest

*An All-Star Team from
the Philadelphia Area*

There is no shortage of outstanding baseball players who have come from the Philadelphia area. Among the legions of players produced in the region, excellent players are in abundance. Many rank among the top echelons of the baseball profession.

A list of the top players—imposing as it is—includes all-time greats of the game, many near greats, and some others who were very, very good. They came from different areas of the region, from different backgrounds, and from different circumstances, and they played with a variety of teams, some good, some not so good.

Subjective though it may be, here's what a Philadelphia-area all-star team would look like (players' birthplaces noted alongside their names):

OF   Reggie Jackson (Wyncote)
OF   Goose Goslin (Salem, NJ)

OF	Del Ennis (Philadelphia)
1B	Mickey Vernon (Marcus Hook)
2B	Eddie Stanky (Philadelphia)
3B	Jimmy Dykes (Philadelphia)
SS	Buck Weaver (Pottstown)
C	Roy Campanella (Philadelphia)
RHP	Bucky Walters (Philadelphia)
LHP	Herb Pennock (Kennett Square)
RP	Ray Narleski (Camden)
UTL	Eddie Miksis (Burlington, NJ)

The group includes four members of the Baseball Hall of Fame (Jackson, Goslin, Campanella, and Pennock). Campanella is a three-time Most Valuable Player, and Jackson and Walters each won the award once. Jackson is a four-time home run champion, and Goslin won a batting title. Also on the list are a two-time batting champion (Vernon), a three-time 20-game winner (Walters), a two-time 20-game winner (Pennock), and RBI champions Ennis, Campanella, Jackson, and Goslin. Dykes was a solid third baseman, Stanky was one of the scrappiest and best leadoff batters of his day, Weaver was an outstanding all-around player, Narleski was a strong pioneering reliever, and Miksis was a masterful utility man.

Here are some brief sketches of their careers:

REGGIE JACKSON

Sometimes, nicknames can be grossly exaggerated. But there was no hyperbole connected with the nickname of Reggie Jackson.

He was called "Mr. October." The moniker might have been a little vain. It might even have been somewhat haughty. But there was never anything overblown about it. Reggie was indeed Mr. October.

Reggie Jackson

That was Jackson's time of the year. He played in 11 League Championship Series. He played in six World Series. Reggie's teams won five of them, and he played a major role in most of them.

Here's just a sampling: He slammed two RBI doubles and scored after singling to give the Oakland Athletics a 3–1 win over the New York Mets in the sixth game of the 1973 World Series. Then he stroked a two-run homer to give the A's a 5–2 win in Game Seven. His home run led the A's to a 3–2 victory over the Los Angeles Dodgers in the first game of the 1974 Series, which was won in five games by Oakland. And in the greatest home run barrage in World Series history, Jackson clouted three successive homers, each on the first pitch, each against a different pitcher, to give the New York Yankees an 8–4 win in the sixth and clinching game of the 1977 Fall Classic.

Overall, the lefthanded Jackson, who hit a memorable 529-foot home run in the 1971 All-Star Game at Tiger Stadium, batted .357 with 10 home runs and 24 RBI in 27 World Series games. His .755 slugging average is the all-time high.

Flamboyant, controversial, and egotistical, Jackson was one of baseball's greatest clutch hitters. He described himself as "the straw that stirs the drink." During his 21 years in the big leagues, he stirred a lot of drinks—and also had a lot of scuffles, most notably with teammate Bill North in the clubhouse and with manager Billy Martin in the dugout before a national television audience. He even had a candy bar named after him.

Jackson grew up in Wyncote and attended Cheltenham High School, where he not only played baseball but was also a fine running back in football. He moved on to Arizona State University, then was a first-round draft choice of the Athletics in 1966. He spent the rest of that year and part of the next in the minors before the A's—then playing in Kansas City—brought him up late in the 1967 season.

The following year the A's moved to Oakland, where Jackson resided until 1975, when as a free agent he moved to the Baltimore Orioles for one season. He then spent five years with the Yankees, five more with the California Angels, then finished his career back in Oakland in 1987.

During his storied career, Jackson, who was elected to the Hall of Fame in 1993, won four home run crowns while hitting a career total of 563, the eighth-highest number in baseball history. He hit more than 30 home runs in seven seasons and had double figures in every season (except 1967) in which he played. His high was 47 in 1969.

He also won three slugging titles and led the league twice in runs scored and once in RBI. Although prone to strikeouts—Reggie holds a number of records in that category—he finished with a .262 batting average. His highest average was in 1980 when he hit .300.

Jackson was the AL's unanimous choice as Most Valuable Player in 1973 when he hit .293 with 32 home runs, 117 RBI, and 99 runs scored, the last three figures being league highs that season. A 14-time member of the AL All-Star team, he was also the MVP in the 1973 and 1977 World Series.

GOOSE GOSLIN

When Leon (Goose) Goslin was a youth growing up on a farm just outside of Salem, New Jersey, he and his friends were called "wharf rats." With school not an important part of their lives, the kids did little else but hang around the wharves of Salem. The rest of the time they played baseball.

Eventually, Goslin played with local sandlot teams while holding a job as a glassblower and later as an elevator mechanic. Goslin was primarily a pitcher in those days, and in 1919 he was signed to his first pro contract on the recommendation of Bill McGowan, a future American League umpire and Wilmington, Del. native.

Ineffective as a minor league pitcher, Goose was quickly converted to an outfielder. In 1921 he won the batting title in the South Atlantic League. Late that season, a few months before his 21st birthday, he was purchased by the Washington Senators. In his first game Goslin delivered a victory to the Senators with a bases-loaded triple.

A lefthanded hitter, Goslin crowded the plate and sometimes had to be told by the umpire to move back. Noted as a superb clutch hitter, he also swung extremely hard. In fact, sometimes he took such a vicious swing that he wound up on his derriere.

Neither habit, however, deterred Goslin from becoming one of the premier hitters of his era. Goose hit .324 in his first full season, and after that hit above .300 10 other times, including seven in a row between 1922 and 1928. He drove in 100 or more runs 11 times. In 1934 he hit safely in 30 straight games, which ties for the

Goose Goslin

13th-longest streak in American League history. The compact 5-foot, 11½-inch, 185 pounder finished his 18-year career in 1938 with a lifetime .316 batting average. He collected 2,735 hits, including 500 doubles, 173 triples, and 248 home runs.

Although he hit .344 in 1924 and .354 in 1926 and led the American League in doubles twice and in RBI once (with 129 in 1924), Goslin's finest season was in 1928. That year, he won the batting championship with a sparkling .379 average. Goose, who led in the race throughout the season, singled in his last at-bat in the ninth inning of the final game of the season to win the title by one point over Heinie Manush of the St. Louis Browns.

A left fielder who was not very adept on defense, Goslin spent his first 10 years with the Senators. He led Washington to its first pennant and World Series victory in 1924, slugging a two-run homer in the second game and four hits including another homer in Game Four, and driving in seven runs overall as the Senators defeated the New York Giants in seven games. Although Washington lost in seven games the following year to the Pittsburgh Pirates, Goslin homered twice, winning the fourth game for Walter Johnson with a two-run blast.

Altogether, Goslin played in five World Series. His Senators bowed to the Giants in five games in 1933. Traded after that season to the Detroit Tigers, he played in the 1934 Series, which the American Leaguers lost in seven games to the St. Louis Cardinals, even though his ninth-inning single won the second game in 12 innings, 3–2. Detroit won its first Series in 1935, defeating the Chicago Cubs in six games with Goslin singling home the winning run in the ninth inning of the final game. Overall, Goose greased opposing pitchers for a .287 average with seven home runs and 18 RBI in 32 World Series games.

Goslin, who once hit into four doubleplays in one game, played five seasons with the Tigers and two with the Browns before finishing his career with his third stint in Washington. He was elected to the Hall of Fame in 1968. For a one-time pitcher, he did pretty well for himself as a slugging outfielder.

DEL ENNIS

In the world of big league baseball, the word "slugger" usually means one thing. It describes a guy who frequently hits the ball out of the park.

On that basis, it is completely within reason to call Del Ennis a slugger. Not only could Ennis hit the ball out of the park, but he did it often. Sometimes the ball was known to fly incredibly long distances.

Ennis hit 288 home runs in a relatively short career of 14 years. While playing with the Philadelphia Phillies for 11 years, he reached double figures every season, blasting 25 or more home runs six times. Del was one of the few players who hit balls onto the roof atop the upper deck in left field at Philadelphia's Shibe Park, later called Connie Mack Stadium. No ordinary slugger ever did that.

As a matter of fact, it was Ennis's power that got him his first pro contract. Phillies scout Jocko Collins watched Ennis wallop two shots completely out of the park and across the tennis courts beyond left field while Del was playing at Olney High School. Initially, Ennis rejected Collins's offers, saying he wasn't good enough to play in the pros. But the veteran scout persevered, and eventually Ennis signed. As a raw 18-year-old, he hit .346 with 18 home runs and 93 RBI at Class B Trenton.

Two years of military service interrupted Del's pro career, but shortly after getting discharged in April 1946, he joined the Phillies. At the end of the year, he had hit .313 and 17 home runs, and was named National League Rookie of the Year by *The Sporting News*.

Ennis was off to the races. By 1949 he had become one of the NL's top sluggers, hitting .302 that year and blasting 25 homers to go along with 110 RBI. But his best was just around the corner. In 1950, Ennis was the key slugger as the Phillies won their first pennant in 35 years. Del led the league with 126 RBI while setting a career high in home runs (31) and batting .311. He drove in seven runs in one game, and three days later drove in seven more, hitting a grand-slam homer in each game. He also went 5-for-10 in a 19-inning Phillies victory over the Cincinnati Reds. Del was a leading candidate for Most Valuable Player, but lost out to Phils relief pitcher Jim Konstanty.

Del Ennis

By the time Ennis was traded by the Phillies to the St. Louis Cardinals after the 1956 season, he was the team's all-time leader in home runs. Even today, he ranks second to Mike Schmidt in that category, is third on the club's list for RBI and total bases, and ranks among the top 10 in virtually all the Phils' other career batting categories.

Philadelphia fans were unjustifiably hard on Ennis, making him a frequent target of their misguided boos. Nevertheless, between 1949 and 1957 Ennis drove in no less than 105 runs in each year but one. He hit .289 in 1952, .285 the following year, and .296 in 1955. He started in two of the three All-Star Games for which he was selected.

Ennis had a good year (.286–24–105) in his first season at St. Louis. But he slowed down after that. He played the final year of his career in 1959 with the Cincinnati Reds and Chicago White Sox. At the relatively young age of 34, saying he was tired of the game, Ennis retired. With him went a slugger who had been one of the league's best for more than a decade.

MICKEY VERNON

It is not unusual for people to come early to the ballpark to watch a particular player take batting practice. In this era of big hitters, it happens all the time. But arriving early to see a guy take fielding practice? No way.

Unless, of course, it was somebody like Mickey Vernon. And if it was, an early arrival was a special treat. With his grace and style, the ultrasmooth first baseman was a sight to behold. Mickey fielded his position with a velvet touch, gliding around the bag as though engaged in a form of outdoor ballet.

Not only was James Barton Vernon one of the most graceful first baseman in history, but he still holds American League career records at that position for games, chances, putouts, and assists and the major league mark for participating in the most doubleplays. He was also a consummate hitter with a textbook swing. Overall, the Marcus Hook native is probably the best first baseman not seated in the Hall of Fame.

During a masterful 20-year career that in going from 1939 to 1960 made Vernon one of the few players to perform in four different decades, Mickey won two batting championships. He led the league in doubles three times. And he laced 2,495 hits while batting .290 or above nine times. He finished with a batting average of .286 with 172 home runs and 1,311 RBI in 2,409 games. Although not a power hitter, he reached a high in home runs with 20 in 1954.

On defense, he led the league in fielding percent-age three times. He had a career mark of .990, three times fielding that same percentage during the season. And with 19,819 chances, Vernon made just 212 errors in his entire career.

Vernon played mostly with the lowly Washington Senators. He got a brief reprieve when he spent one and one-half years with the Cleveland Indians and two seasons with the Boston Red Sox before suiting up for Washington again, the Milwaukee Braves, and the Pittsburgh Pirates at the end of his career.

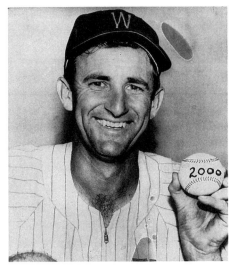

Mickey Vernon

A graduate of Eddystone High School, Mickey attended Villanova University for one year, after which he and his hometown buddy Danny Murtaugh signed in 1937 with a Class D team in Easton, Maryland, that was affiliated with the St. Louis Browns.

After his first minor league season, Vernon was signed by the Senators. He spent another one and one-half seasons in the minors before getting summoned to the Senators in 1939. Mickey became the club's regular first baseman in 1941.

In 1946, after two years of military service, Vernon ran away with the AL batting crown, hitting a lofty .353, 11 points ahead of second-place Ted Williams. Then, after hitting .306 in 1950, the seven-time All-Star team member won his second batting title in 1953 when he went down to the wire to edge the Indians' Al Rosen, who was bidding for a Triple Crown, by one point with a .337 average.

Vernon was the favorite player of President Dwight Eisenhower and one of the most popular players in Washington history. In his native Delaware County, he is virtually treated as a deity. Whether it was with the glove or with the bat, the gentlemanly Vernon was equal to the popularity his performance commanded.

EDDIE STANKY

Although he stood just 5 feet, 8 inches, it was never good policy to underestimate Eddie Stanky. He was a guy who could beat an opponent in a variety of ways, and if he didn't do it with his playing, he'd do it with his head.

Stanky was the kind of player who drove opponents crazy. He was a scrapper. He was brash, aggressive, intelligent. He clawed and he hustled, and when he had to do it, he was not averse to a little fisticuffs. He wasn't nicknamed "The Brat" for his mild manner.

Eddie was a respectable fielder, and as a leadoff man he was no pushover at the plate. He had a career batting average of .268, twice hitting .300 or more, and he fielded to a .978 tune, not too shabby for a second baseman. In a moment of hyperbole, Leo Durocher once said of Stanky: "He can't hit, he can't run, and he can't field. But I wouldn't trade him for any second baseman in the National League."

If there was one thing that was Stanky's strong point, though, it was his ability to get on base. An extremely skilled manipulator of his bat, "Muggsy," as he was also called, could draw a base on balls as easily as riding a bicycle to the corner candy store. The tough little second baseman led the league in walks three times, reaching a high of 148 in 1945, then a major league record. In his six seasons as a regular, he always walked more than 100 times. In 1950 he walked seven straight times, tying a major league record.

Eddie suited up with the Chicago Cubs, Brooklyn Dodgers, Boston Braves, New York Giants, and St. Louis Cardinals. He played with three pennant winners—the Dodgers in 1947, Braves in 1948,

Eddie Stanky

and Giants in 1951. Overall, he played in 11 seasons from 1943 to 1953. In several seasons serious injuries, including a broken leg, kept him from playing the full campaign. In 1950, when he hit .300 and led the league with 144 walks, Stanky placed third in the NL in the voting for Most Valuable Player.

Stanky grew up in the Kensington section of Philadelphia and graduated from the original Northeast High School at Eighth Street and Lehigh Avenue, just 13 blocks from Shibe Park. Soccer was his first love, and he was very good at it as a schoolboy in the one area of the city that avidly played and followed the sport.

But baseball was also on Stanky's list of popular endeavors, and after graduation, despite a .234 batting average as a senior, the youngster was signed by the Philadelphia Athletics. Stanky was shipped to Class C Greenville (Mississippi), but after a few weeks there, discouraged and homesick, he wrote to his mother to send him money to come home.

Mom Stanky refused her son's request, telling him that she "didn't want any quitters in the family." So Stanky stayed. And for the next eight years he wandered around the minor leagues. Finally, after hitting above .300 in three straight years for Macon, the manager, Milt Stock, who would become Eddie's father-in-law, sold his contract to Milwaukee, a Triple-A team in the American Association that belonged to the Cubs. After hitting .342 and getting named the league's Most Valuable Player, Stanky moved up to the Cubs in 1943.

Classified 4-F because of a hearing problem, he was not drafted for World War II, but kept playing ball. He wound up in Brooklyn in mid-1944, and the following year led the league with 128 runs. Two years later, Stanky was one of the few Dodgers who stood up for Jackie Robinson when he joined the club (later, as a manager, he taunted Robinson). Eddie had his best year in 1948 when he hit .320 to help the Braves win the National League pennant.

JIMMY DYKES

In the days of yesteryear, Philadelphia was seldom without a hometown player who performed for the local team and who was popular with the fans. Jimmy Dykes was a perfect example.

Dykes, who born in Philadelphia, then raised in Oakmont in Delaware County and graduated in 1914 from Haverford High School, where he was a catcher, started his career with the Athletics, and he never really left town. He lived there in the off-season, even when he played with other teams, and stayed around the city for his entire life. In the process, he developed legions of friends and fans, making him a huge favorite of the local populace.

Self-described as "roly-poly," the 5-foot, 9-inch, 185 pounder wore the colors of big league teams for 22 seasons, 16 as a regular. He was a member of Athletics teams that won three pennants and two World Series between 1929 and 1931, and he was the starting American League third baseman in 1933 in the first All-Star Game.

Dykes was primarily a third baseman, but he also held down second base at various times. He holds the American League for most chances (17) by a second baseman in a nine-inning game. Jimmy played an occasional shortstop and first base, appeared once in a

Jimmy Dykes

great while in the outfield, and even pitched in two games. He was an adequate but not spectacular defensive player.

He was, however, a solid everyday hitter. And he was tough and aggressive, and he never stopped hustling. Among a galaxy of superstars with Hall of Fame credentials on the Athletics, he blended in perfectly.

The cigar-chomping Dykes logged just one season in the minors before making his big league debut with the A's in 1918. That season was interrupted by military service, but returning in 1919, Dykes spent the start of the year with the A's before playing most of the season with Atlanta in the Southern League.

In 1920, Dykes was back with the Athletics to stay. With the exception of one season shortened by injury, he was a regular for the next 13 years. He hit higher than .300 five times, going .312 in 1924, .323 in 1925, .324 in 1927, .327 in 1929, and .301 in 1930. Overall, he hit .270 or more 11 times as a regular.

In 18 games in three World Series, Jimmy hit .288. He ripped two singles in the famous 10-run seventh inning staged by the Athletics in their comeback win over the Chicago Cubs in the fourth game of the 1929 Series. His two-run homer helped the A's to victory over the St. Louis Cardinals in the sixth and clinching game of the 1930 Series.

As he too often did with his star players, Connie Mack sold Dykes, Al Simmons, and Mule Haas to the Chicago White Sox after the 1932 season for a reported $150,000. That deal ended Jimmy's long career in Philadelphia and began a new one in Chicago, where he spent the next six of seven seasons as a player-manager and 12-plus years altogether as the Chisox skipper.

Dykes came to the plate for his final at-bat in 1939. When his playing career ended, he had hit .280 with 108 home runs, 1,071 RBI, and 1,108 runs scored in 2,282 games. That record was more than enough to earn the approval of the local fans.

BUCK WEAVER

Although a tragic figure who was involved in the infamous "Black Sox" scandal of 1919 and subsequently banned from baseball for life, Buck Weaver was an outstanding player who was possibly headed for the Hall of Fame. Despite his troubles, Weaver wins the nod as the Philadelphia area's best shortstop.

The selection is somewhat skewed because Weaver really wins the honor by default. There are no other shortstops from the region who come anywhere near the Pottstown native's credentials.

And Weaver himself was more recognized as a third baseman than he was as a shortstop. In actuality, though, Buck played nearly twice as many games at shortstop during his nine-year major league career as he did at third base. He performed at short in 822 games and at third in 426 contests.

George Daniel Weaver was the regular shortstop with the Chicago White Sox in his first four years in the majors (1912 through 1915). He divided his time between short and third in 1916, then became the team's starting shortstop again in 1918. It was only in 1917 and then in his last two years—1919 and 1920—that Buck was Chicago's regular third baseman.

A righthanded batter, Weaver had a career batting average of .272. He hit .300, .296, and .333 in his final three years. Never a long-distance slugger, he clubbed only 21 home runs during his career, but slammed 33 doubles one season and 35 the next. He drove in a total of 420 runs while scoring 623. Buck led the American League in at-bats in 1919 with 571.

The always-smiling, popular Weaver excelled defensively. A sure-handed glove man, he was often described as a cat, because of the way he pounced on ground balls. In his final years he was regarded as the finest-fielding third baseman in baseball. He was said to have been the only third sacker that Ty Cobb refused to bunt on.

21

Despite his many talents, however, the kid who grew up in Stowe, just outside of Pottstown where he attended the local high school, is mostly known as one of eight White Sox who dumped the 1919 World Series, the club losing five games to three to the Cincinnati Reds. Although a Grand Jury in Chicago exonerated the group, all eight players who were alleged to have taken bribes were banned for life from baseball by commissioner Kenesaw Mountain Landis following the 1920 season.

Weaver, who hit .324 in the Series and who was in the prime of his career, steadfastly maintained his innocence, claiming he never accepted any money to help throw the Series. He was, however, ac-

Buck Weaver

cused of failing to reveal the plot to the proper authorities, despite knowing that the fix was taking place.

Buck spent the rest of his life attempting to clear his name and to get reinstated in baseball. He never succeeded.

ROY CAMPANELLA

As the story goes, when Roy Campanella was a sturdy teenager growing up in the Nicetown section of Philadelphia, he frequently appeared at Shibe Park to ask for a tryout. He was always rejected, by both the Phillies and the Athletics, because back then major league baseball did not allow African American players among its ranks.

For that unconscionable reason, Philadelphia was deprived of one of its greatest local treasures. Ultimately, Philadelphia's loss was Brooklyn's gain. Campy, who had been rejected by other teams as well, went on to a Hall of Fame career during which he won three Most Valuable Player awards and was the heart and soul of the great Dodgers teams of the 1950s.

Any list of baseball's top five catchers includes the name Campanella. The stocky, 5-foot, 9-inch, 205 pounder was not only a powerful hitter, but also a quick and agile catcher with a rifle throwing arm. Moreover, he was an expert handler of pitchers.

Unfortunately, the one-time student at Simon Gratz High School had a big league career that started too late and ended too soon. He spent just 10 years in the majors before an auto accident ended his career. At the time he had a career batting average of .276 with 242 home runs and 856 RBI.

Campy had started in professional baseball as a 15-year-old in 1937, playing with the Baltimore Elite Giants in the Negro National League in the summer and in Latin America in the winter. Ten years after he began, Roy became one of the first black players— and the first black catcher—to integrate organized baseball when

Roy Campanella

he signed a contract in 1946 to play with the Dodgers' Nashua farm team in the New England League. After one and one-half seasons in Triple-A ball with Montreal and St. Paul, Campanella joined the Dodgers in 1948 as only the third black player in the big leagues.

He quickly became the team leader and one of its best hitters. He hit over .300 three times, drilled more than 30 home runs four times, and on three occasions drove in more than 100 runs. Along the way, he was voted the National League's Most Valuable Player in 1951, 1953, and 1955. And he was a member of eight NL All-Star teams.

Campanella's first big season was in 1951 when he hit .325 with 33 homers and 108 RBI. In 1953 he hit .312 while slamming 41 home runs and a league-leading 142 RBI, both then-records for a catcher. In 1955 he went .310–32–107. Roy led Dodger teams to five pennants and one World Series victory. In Series play he hit just .237 with four home runs and 12 RBI in 32 games. But Campy was behind the plate when Johnny Podres hurled the Dodgers to their first Series victory in 1955.

He was behind the plate for hundreds of other important games, even though he was suffering injuries that would have sidelined lesser men. But the robust backstop never complained. The guy with the big offense and the equally big defense kept rolling along. Once he even stole home to give the Dodgers a 12-inning victory.

His career ended just as the Dodgers were getting ready to move to Los Angeles. While he was driving to his home on Long Island, his car slipped on an icy road and overturned. Roy survived, but he was paralyzed from the neck down. One year later a Roy Campanella Night was held in the Los Angeles Coliseum for an exhibition game between the Dodgers and Yankees. The game drew 93,103 spectators, the largest attendance at one game in major league history.

Although his career was over, Campy will forever be regarded as one of baseball's finest catchers.

BUCKY WALTERS

The fields of baseball have not exactly been cluttered with mediocre position players who became successful pitchers. But sometimes the conversion happens. Sometimes it even works.

In the case of Bucky Walters, he was a third baseman who excelled as a pitcher. He did so well, in fact, that he was a 20-game winner three times, led the National League in complete games

Bucky Walters

and innings pitched three times, in ERA twice, and in strikeouts once. And, by the way, he was the National League's Most Valuable Player in 1939.

Walters, who was raised in Mt. Airy and attended Germantown High School, had no thoughts of being a pitcher when he came off the sandlots to sign a minor league contract in 1929. He was a fine hitter and third baseman—and also a noted basketball player who, in his early baseball days, also performed in the Eastern League with a team called the Elks. Bucky spent five years in the minors, once hitting as high as .326 for a Williamsport team managed by Glenn Killinger, later the legendary football coach at West Chester State College.

He played briefly with the Boston Braves in 1931, then made trips between the Braves, the Boston Red Sox, and the minors over the next three years. Walters never hit much, and in 1934 he was sold to the Philadelphia Phillies. That season, he manned the hot corner in 80 games with the Phillies, hitting a respectable .260.

But Phils manager Jimmie Wilson had other ideas. He saw a player who had little future as an infielder but who had a great arm. After some prodding, Wilson convinced Walters that he should be a pitcher. Bucky had toed the rubber briefly in 1929 in his first year in the minors, but had not done it since. He worked in two games in 1934, then became a full-time hurler the following year.

Bucky's development came slowly. After going 9–9 his first year, he led the league in losses with an 11–21 record in 1936. Two years later, the Phillies, always in need of cash, sent Walters to the Cincinnati Reds for two players and $55,000. It may have been one of the best moves the Reds ever made.

With a good team, Walters quickly blossomed into one of the top hurlers in the league. In his first full season in 1939 he combined with Paul Derringer to win 52 games and led the Reds to the National League pennant. Bucky led the league in wins with a 27–11 record, in complete games, innings pitched, strikeouts, and ERA.

After the season, he was named the league's MVP. The following year, Walters again led the league in ERA, innings, complete games, and wins (22–10) as Cincinnati won its second straight pennant. After getting swept by the New York Yankees in the '39 World Series, the Reds beat the Detroit Tigers in seven games in the '40 Series with Bucky pitching a three-hit, 5–3 win in the second game, and a five-hit, 4–0 shutout in Game Six.

Despite some slippage in the standings by the Reds, Walters continued his outstanding pitching, winning 72 games over the next four years, including 19 in 1941 and a league-leading 23 in 1944. That season, he fired a one-hitter against the Braves, yielding only a two-out, eighth-inning single to Connie Ryan.

Bucky hurt his arm during the 1945 season and was never right after that. He won just 28 games over a three-year period before retiring and becoming the Reds manager in 1948. The five-time All-Star pitched one game in 1950, finishing his career with a 198–160 record with a 3.30 ERA in 428 games. Not bad for an ex–third baseman.

HERB PENNOCK

Among today's 90-mile-per-hour rocketeers, there would probably be no place for Herb Pennock. He was not one who would launch blazing missiles, then retire to the clubhouse, assured that he'd done a good job after throwing 100 pitches.

No sir, there was no pampering of Pennock, or for that matter any of his colleagues of the day. Pennock would go out and start game after game, pitching inning after inning, completing games, winning games, and generally hurling superbly during his 22-year career.

Pennock was not a fastball pitcher. In fact, his pitches were often so slow they were compared to basketballs as they floated to the plate. But the slender lefthander who was known for his smooth,

Herb Pennock

effortless delivery had several kinds of curves, a change-up, and a screwball. He was cunning. Also a perfectionist, he had a vast knowledge of the hitters, and he could outsmart them as easily as buttoning up his vest. He threw both sidearm and overhand. And he had control.

The native of Kennett Square did not come by his control easily. Plagued initially by chronic wildness, he worked on his control by regularly throwing batting practice before games. During the off-season he threw at barn doors and stone walls.

Pennock's diligence paid off. In 3,571 innings pitched, he walked just 916 batters while striking out 1,227. His record was 241–162 with a 3.60 ERA in 617 games. He was also credited later with 33 saves. Pennock was elected to the Hall of Fame in 1948.

Herb, who had attended Cedarcroft Academy, in Unionville, Pa., had his heart set on matriculating at the University of Pennsylvania. But he was dissuaded from that goal when he was signed in 1912 as an 18-year-old by the Philadelphia Athletics. Although Connie Mack wanted Pennock to sit and watch, he wound up using Herb in relief two days after his arrival, and the kid allowed one hit in four innings. One year later, the young lefty beat the Detroit Tigers, 1–0, in the game that clinched the American League pennant for the A's. Pennock also nearly became the first pitcher to toss a no-hitter on opening day when he one-hit the Boston Red Sox in 1915.

In one of his many misguided moves, Mack sold Pennock to the Red Sox during the 1915 season, even though the youngster had shown great promise, especially after posting an 11–4 record in 1914. Pennock stayed with Boston through the 1922 season, winning 60 games, including 16 twice in succession. Ironically, Pennock gave up both the first and last home runs that Babe Ruth hit in the Polo Grounds, where the New York Yankees played before they moved to Yankee Stadium.

In 1923, "The Squire of Kennett Square," as he was called, was acquired by the Yankees for three players and $50,000. Pennock was an immediate success. He registered a 19–6 mark, then went 21–9, 16–17, 23–11, 19–8, and 17–6.

The Yankees won the pennant and World Series in Pennock's first year with them. Herb won the second game and the deciding sixth game to launch a remarkable Series run. He hurled in three more World Series, winning the first and fifth games in a seven-game Yankees victory in 1926, and firing a Game Three three-hitter for a win in the Yankees sweep in 1927. In 10 outings altogether, he rang up a remarkable 5–0 record with a sparkling 1.95 ERA. He is the only pitcher to twirl that many Series games and be undefeated.

Pennock, who also pitched without a decision in the 1932 Series, left the Yankees after the 1933 campaign. He finished his career the following year back with the Red Sox. Later, he became the general manager of the Philadelphia Phillies.

RAY NARLESKI

There is nothing unusual today about teams employing both right-handed and lefthanded relief pitchers. But there was a time when that practice didn't exist. Ray Narleski was one of the pioneers who took part in changing that formula.

Narleski was a righthander. In the mid-1950s he teamed with southpaw Don Mossi to give the Cleveland Indians what was essentially baseball's first left-right bullpen combination.

The hard-throwing Camden native and graduate of Collingswood High School wasn't always a reliever. The Indians had signed him in 1948, and through the early part of his six-year minor league stint—with one year spent at home after he quit in a salary dispute—Narleski was a starter. He was switched to relief, despite his objections, in 1953. For the rest of his career, Ray resided in the bullpen.

Narleski, whose father Bill was an infielder for two years with the Boston Red Sox, made it up to the Indians in 1954. That happened to be the year in which Cleveland had assembled one of the best pitching staffs in baseball history. It included future Hall of Famers Bob Feller, Early Wynn, Bob Lemon, and Hal Newhouser. It was also the year in which the Indians set a record at that time with 111 wins.

Anxious to give his starters an occasional break, the astute Cleveland manager Al Lopez paired Narleski and Mossi in the bullpen, each pitching according to the situation. They also took turns as closers.

Teams had had only one main reliever in the past. But no one had ever had a right-left combination used in key situations be-

Ray Narleski

fore. It was the start of a whole new approach to the process of relieving.

Narleski went 3–3 with 13 saves and a 2.22 ERA in 42 games in his rookie year. In one game, he, Mike Garcia, and Wynn combined to pitch a one-hitter against the Chicago White Sox, the only safety coming on Minnie Minoso's ninth-inning single off Wynn. In 1955 he upped his workload to a league-leading 60 games, posting a 9–1 record with 19 saves, also a league best. At one point, he toiled in 38 straight innings without allowing a run. During that streak, he trudged to the mound nine games in a row.

After a 3–2, four-save, 1.52 ERA season in 1956 that was curtailed by back problems, Ray bounced back with an 11–5 mark and 16 saves in 1957. Still hoping to become a starter, he got his chance, and was on the mound at the beginning of 15 of his 46 games.

With Cleveland in need of starters again in 1958, Narleski was called on to make 24 starts. In 44 games overall, he registered a 13–10 record. That turned out to be Ray's last season with the Indians. After a midwinter contract dispute with general manager Frank Lane, Narleski was traded—amazingly with Mossi—to the Detroit Tigers. Returning mostly to the bullpen, Ray went 4–12 with five saves in 42 games.

His back ailment continued to give him problems, however, and when the Tigers tried to send Narleski back to the minors, he refused to report or to accept a minor league contract. Instead, he retired from the big leagues, bringing home with him a 43–33 career record with 58 saves and a 3.60 ERA in 266 games.

EDDIE MIKSIS

It is a special luxury to have a player who can fill in at a number of different positions. He is often called a jack-of-all-trades. Some teams have such a player. To their disadvantage, others don't.

The Brooklyn Dodgers and Chicago Cubs were among the lucky ones. They had Eddie Miksis. He could play third base, second base, shortstop, or even the outfield or first base. And he could pinch-hit or pinch-run. Indeed, Miksis was the ultimate utility man.

He played each position, whichever it happened to be, to the fullest. No manager was ever reluctant to insert Miksis into the lineup. He was always useful. As one writer put it, "Miksis'll fix us." Over a 14-year period, Eddie played in 1,042 games. Some 382 were at second base, 219 at third base, and 137 at shortstop. He hit .236 with 44 home runs.

Miksis was a Burlington, New Jersey, native who attended Burlington High School, where he was also an outstanding basketball player. He broke into the pro ranks at Trenton in 1944, and before the season was over he had moved up to the Dodgers. At the time Eddie was 18 years old.

The speedy Miksis played in 26 games at Brooklyn in 1944, after which he spent the better part of two years in the military before returning to the Dodgers late in the 1946 season. He then plied his versatility with the great Brooklyn teams until he was traded to the Cubs in mid-1951 in a blockbuster deal involving eight players.

While he played with the Dodgers, Miksis appeared in two World Series. He was the pinch-runner who scored the winning run when Cookie Lavagetto's pinch-hit double broke up the no-hit bid of the New York Yankees' Floyd (Bill) Bevens in the bottom of the ninth inning of the fourth game of a memorable 1947 World Series.

After switching to the Cubs, Miksis shed his utility role. He became the team's regular second baseman during three of the next four years, and later started as an outfielder. All the while, of course, he also put in some hours at third base and shortstop.

Miksis spent five and one-half years in Chicago. He reached a career high in 1951 with a .265 batting average while playing in 121 games Two years later he appeared in 142 games, playing mostly second base but also some at shortstop. In 1956, Eddie's fifth full year with Chicago, he was moved to center field because of a knee injury and was a regular at that position. Overall, Miksis, who once lined a drive off Willie Mays's head for a double, played in 142 games that season.

Following the 1956 campaign, Miksis was traded to the St. Louis Cardinals, where he resumed his role as a utility man. He then played with the Baltimore Orioles and the Cincinnati Reds, retiring after the 1958 season.

By the time he finished his ca-

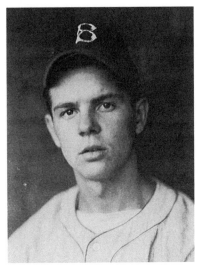

Eddie Miksis

reer, Miksis was known as one of the most valuable and versatile utility men in baseball. As a starter, he was a solid everyday player who was heavily steeped in the fundamentals of the game. Eddie had many memorable experiences—including his participation in three no-hitters—and most of all, his dash home in one of the most exciting World Series ever played.

2 Some Stayed Home

They Played with the Phillies or Athletics

In 1952 little Bobby Shantz had a season that would have made a giant proud. The 5-foot, 6-inch, 140-pound lefthander posted a 24–7 record in one of the most spectacular feats ever accomplished by a player so small.

Although he pitched for a fifth-place Philadelphia Athletics team that finished 16 games out of first place, Shantz was rewarded for his magnificent work by being named the American League's Most Valuable Player. Not only was it an honor that the elfin southpaw richly deserved, but it was also the last significant accomplishment by an A's pitcher before the team was spirited away to Kansas City two years later.

Shantz's record, which included a sparkling 2.48 ERA, probably would've been even better had he not been hit by a pitch (thrown by Philadelphian Walt Masterson of the Washington Senators) and suffered a broken wrist that forced him to miss the final three weeks of the season. As it turned out, though, Shantz became only

Bobby Shantz

the fifth American League hurler to win an MVP award and the third of four Philadelphia-area natives to win the honor.

Many years later, Shantz would claim that his wondrous season was "just one of those years when everything went right." That it did. Bobby, a 4-foot, 11-inch outfielder in his senior year at Potts-town High School, won nearly one-third of his team's total victories. He added to his lustrous season when he struck out the side—Whitey Lockman, Jackie Robinson, and Stan Musial—in the All-Star Game played that year at Philadelphia's Shibe Park.

Although Shantz never had another year like he did in 1952, he spent 16 productive seasons in the big leagues between 1949 and 1964. In his rookie season, he had pitched nine innings of hitless re-lief before yielding a 13th-inning safety in a game with the Detroit Tigers. After leaving the Athletics, his best years were with the New York Yankees, a team that converted him to full-time relief pitch-ing, a role in which he continued to serve through much of the rest of his career. Bobby, who was twice picked in expansion drafts—he was the winning pitcher in the Houston Colt 45s' first home game in 1962—finished with a 119–99 career record and a 3.38 ERA. He worked in 537 games, including the last ones with the Phillies.

Like Shantz, many other fine players began life in the Philadel-phia area and stayed around to wear the uniforms of either the Ath-letics or the Phillies. Some of the local boys who made good locally forged outstanding careers that rank among the finest in the history of their respective teams.

One such player is Harry Davis, the gentlemanly slugging first baseman and first captain of the Athletics. Lost among the modern day multitudes of professional baseball players and a 30-team ma-jor league, the Philadelphia-born Davis was one of the city's first great power hitters in the 20th century.

Davis is one of two native sons (the other being Reggie Jackson) who won four major league home run titles. Although playing in the dead-ball era, the Girard College graduate topped the American

Harry Davis

League in homers each year between 1904 and 1907, thus becoming the young circuit's first bona fide home run king. His numbers never exceeded 12 in a season, but Davis was in his day an exceptional long-distance clouter who also led the league in doubles three times, reaching a career high in 1905 with 47. In addition, he led the AL twice in RBI and once in runs scored. One of his RBI in 1906 ended a major league record of 48 consecutive scoreless innings played by the Athletics.

On the small side for a first baseman of today at 5 feet, 10 inches, 180 pounds, Davis—nicknamed Jasper—attended Lehigh University before beginning his pro career in 1895 as an outfielder in the National League with the New York Giants. He played with three other NL teams, including Connie Mack's Pittsburgh Pirates, before jumping in 1901 to Mack's Athletics in the newly formed American League. The captain of three A's pennant winners, Davis was an astute player known particularly for his ability to steal the other team's signs.

He spent 16 of the next 17 years with his hometown team, leaving only briefly in 1912 to manage the Cleveland Spiders before returning to the A's the following year to finish his career as a reserve. During a 22-year career that ended in 1917, Davis hit .277 with 75 home runs and 951 RBI. A fine fielder and base stealer, he hit above .300 three times as a regular with the A's, his high coming in 1904 when he hit .309.

Another exceptional player who stayed home was Norristown's Roy Thomas, a dandy center fielder who played 13 seasons between 1899 and 1911, including his first nine and last two with the Phillies.

A University of Pennsylvania graduate, Thomas jumped from the Quakers directly to the Phillies. At the time, *The Sporting News* called him "the greatest amateur player of his generation." In his first season he set a National League record for a rookie by scoring 137 runs.

Thomas was a superb leadoff man. And he was a master at fouling away pitches. In a game in 1900 he was rewarded with a punch by Cincinnati Reds pitcher Bill Phillips after he had fouled off 12 pitches in one at-bat. Roy led the league in bases on balls seven times, including five years in a row. He also led the league in runs scored once with 131 in 1900, while scoring more than 100 runs four times. His lifetime batting average was .290, which included five seasons over .300. Thomas, who hit just seven home runs during his career, had a career-high batting average of .327 in 1903.

Along with his offensive skills, Thomas, who coached baseball at Penn and Haverford College after his playing career ended, was a fine defensive player. He led National League outfielders in fielding percentage five times and in putouts twice.

Catcher Jimmie Wilson was also a special hometown star. Wilson was an enormously popular player, who put in two stints with the Phillies, the second as player-manager. The Kensington-bred Wilson's first love was soccer. He was playing professionally in Bethlehem when it occurred to

Roy Thomas

him that hitting, throwing, and catching balls held a more promising future than kicking them.

Wilson eventually joined the Phillies in 1923, and in the ensuing years he became one of the National League's premier catchers. Twice an All-Star, including as a starter in 1935, Wilson played from 1923 to 1928 and from 1933 to 1938 with the Phillies. Overall, he played in 18 seasons, making stops with the St. Louis Cardinals and Cincinnati Reds and playing in four World Series. Pressed into

Danny Murphy

service in the 1940 Series won by the Reds, Wilson, then a 40-year-old coach, hit .353 in six of the seven games and even stole the only base of the Series.

With four seasons over .300, including .325 in 1929, Wilson wound up with a .284 career batting average. He hit 32 home runs and drove in 621. Along with being a fine hitter, Wilson was also an outstanding defensive catcher.

Also from an earlier time when players were more likely to play with their hometown teams than they are today was Danny Murphy, who was born in Philadelphia but spent his formative years in Norwich, Connecticut. A .289 hitter during 16 years in the big leagues, Murphy played from 1900 to 1915, beginning his career with the Giants, ending it with the Brooklyn Brookfeds in the Federal League, and in between spending 12 highly productive years with the Athletics.

Murphy went 6-for-6 in his Athletics debut in 1902 and 4-for-5 in the first game at Shibe Park in 1909. Succeeding Davis as the A's captain, the genial Murphy helped the A's win five American League pennants, hitting as high as .329 in 1911. He was a second baseman throughout the first half of his career, but when the A's signed future Hall of Fame second sacker Eddie Collins, Murphy moved to right field, where he stayed the rest of his playing days. He finished with 44 home runs and 702 RBI and at the peak of his career was an accomplished base stealer.

Another captain of the Athletics was Amos Strunk, who grew up in Philadelphia's Strawberry Mansion section, where he played as a youth with the Park Sparrows. A graduate of Central Manual Train-

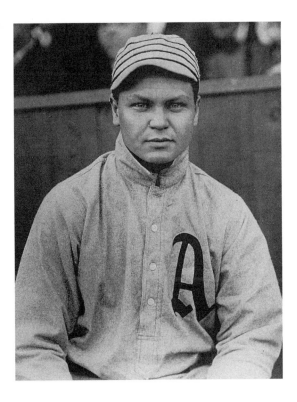

Amos Strunk

ing School, the speedy Strunk was a major leaguer for 17 seasons from 1908 through 1924, including the first 10 years and later parts of three other seasons with the Athletics.

The hard-hitting outfielder spent five years as a regular with the A's, hitting as high as .316 in 1916. Strunk, an exceptional defensive player who led American League outfielders in fielding percentage a major-league-record five times, hit .332 for the Chicago White Sox in 1921 and compiled a lifetime average of .284. He played in four World Series with the Athletics and one with the Boston Red Sox.

Also with the Athletics for most of his career was outfielder Bris Lord of Upland in Delaware County. Lord hit .256 in eight years between 1905 and 1913. He hit .310 with the 1913 A's before winding up with a .256 mark. He was also stationed in the outfield for A's pennant winners in 1905, 1910, and 1911, the latter two being World Series winners.

Another Philadelphia player from long ago was shortstop Montford Montgomery (Monte) Cross, a veteran of 15 big league seasons, 11 of them as a starter. Cross was one of that small group of local boys who not only grew up to play for his hometown team, but played for both of them.

Although he entered the majors in 1892 and played for three National League teams over the next six seasons, Cross joined the Phillies in 1898 and for the next four years was their regular shortstop. A weak hitter—he batted .234 in 1,682 big league games—Cross also had his flaws in the field. In his first season with the Phillies he made 93 errors. He followed that with 90 miscues in 1899. After jumping to the American League in 1902, Cross played with the Athletics through 1907. He reached a career low at the plate in 1904 when he hit .189 in 153 games.

Bill McCahan was the last Philadelphia-area native to toss a no-hitter. The Philadelphia Athletics' righthander did it in 1947, blanking Washington, 3–0. Only one batter reached base against McCahan, that coming on a throwing error by Ferris Fain.

Born in Philadelphia, McCahan moved out of the city as a youth and graduated from what was then called Langhorne High School. He was also a graduate of Duke University and an instructor pilot on a bomber during World War II. A fastball pitcher, McCahan joined the Athletics in 1946, but except for the following year when he posted a 10–5 record, was victimized by arm trouble and never lived up to his promise. His big league career ended in 1949, although he later tried an unsuccessful comeback with the Brooklyn Dodgers. McCahan's career record was 16–14 in 57 games.

Several other players from many years ago joined the march from the local sandlots to the Athletics. One was catcher Jack Lapp, a Frazer native who spent eight of his nine big league seasons with the A's. Lapp hit .263 as a backup catcher with the A's from 1908 through 1915. Woodbury, New Jersey, pitcher Carroll Brown, owner of the colorful nickname "Boardwalk," fashioned a 17–11 record in 1913 while winning 33 games (losing 29) between 1911 and 1914 with the Athletics. In one of his less praiseworthy outings, Brown walked 15 batters in seven and two-thirds innings in a 1913 game, but still got a 16–9 win for the A's over the Tigers.

There was a time toward the later part of the 20th century when the Phillies shunned local players, largely because team officials thought that playing for the hometown team put too much pressure on the athletes. But the club was seldom without a hometown boy during many of the earlier years.

A small cluster of localites was particularly prominent on local teams in the early 1940s. Two natives of Chester, Phillies second baseman Danny Murtaugh and pitcher Johnny Podgajny, were parts of that group.

Bill McCahan

Murtaugh led the National League in stolen bases—with the unfathomably low number of 18—in his rookie season in 1941. Danny, although originally signed by the St. Louis Browns, played his first three big league seasons with the Phillies before entering military service and eventually going on to a nine-year playing career (.254 batting average) that included stints with the Boston Braves and Pittsburgh Pirates, and an outstanding career as a manager. Pod-

Hal Wagner

Jack Meyer

gajny won 20 games for the Phils between 1940 and 1943 en route to a 20–37 overall mark that reached its conclusion in 1946.

Another player who began his career with the Phillies was Rick Schu, who spent the first four of his eight-plus seasons with them. Schu was born in Philadelphia but grew up in California. The Phils' regular third baseman in 1985, Schu hit .246 for his career.

Catcher Hal Wagner, a one-time student at Duke, was a Riverton, New Jersey, native who first appeared with the Athletics in 1937, then stayed with the team as a backup until 1944. Wagner was the starting catcher on the American League champion Red Sox in 1946, then played with the Detroit Tigers before ending his career with the Phillies in 1949 with a .248 career average. Philadelphian Al Brancato was the Athletics' regular shortstop in 1940 and 1941 during four seasons with the A's. He had a career mark of .214. Another member of this local group was former La Salle College basketball star Frank

Hoerst, who logged a 10–33 record with the Phillies in five seasons surrounding World War II.

Yet another player who made a big name for himself before signing with the Phillies was Jack Meyer, who while pitching at Penn Charter was one of the finest schoolboy hurlers in Philadelphia annals. The flame-throwing Meyer became a standout reliever for the Phils, leading the National League in saves with 16 in his rookie year in 1955. In 202 games—178 in relief—Meyer registered a 24–34 record before a back injury forced him to retire in 1961. Meyer, who struck out nearly one batter per inning during his career, once fanned the first six batters he faced (a major league record) after entering a game in relief.

Another Penn Charter alumnus from Philadelphia is Ruben Amaro, Jr., the current assistant general manager of the Phillies.

Ruben Amaro, Jr.

The Stanford University graduate began his pro career in 1991 with the California Angels, but he soon returned to Philadelphia, joining the Phillies in 1992. Overall, he spent five seasons with the Phillies sandwiched around two years with the Cleveland Indians. Amaro was a member of the pennant-winning Phillies in 1993 and the American League champion Indians in 1995. Primarily a reserve outfielder and pinch-hitter, he compiled a lifetime batting average of .235 during eight big league seasons.

3 Standouts from the Surrounding Area

Top Players from the Philadelphia Suburbs,
South Jersey, and Northern Delaware

There are no monuments in Croydon that mark the birthplace of Ray Caldwell. Maybe there should be. Caldwell was once not only a top pitcher, but also one of baseball's most colorful players, whose 12-year major league career was filled with unusual experiences.

Caldwell pitched a no-hitter. He was a 20-game winner. He was one of baseball's last legal spitball pitchers. He roomed briefly with Babe Ruth. And he was once struck by lightning during a game, but recovered to finish it.

During a career that reached from 1910 through 1921, Caldwell posted a 134–120 record while pitching for the New York Highlanders (later to be renamed Yankees), Boston Red Sox, and Cleveland Indians. Nicknamed "Rube" and "Slim," he had a career ERA of 3.22 while working in 343 games.

Caldwell was the Yankees' best pitcher in 1914 and 1915 when he went 18–9 and 19–16, respectively, for second-division clubs.

Ray Caldwell

After four seasons of winning in double figures, Caldwell was traded to the Red Sox, where he became Ruth's roommate. Soon thereafter, he was amazingly released and wound up in Cleveland, where in his Indians debut he had a 2–1 lead over the Philadelphia Athletics when a violent thunderstorm hit League Park with two outs in the ninth inning. Caldwell was knocked to the ground by a bolt of lightning. After several minutes he was revived, and with the storm passing quickly, he returned to the mound to record the last out.

Late in the 1919 season Caldwell tossed a no-hitter, beating the Yankees, 3–0. Just two years earlier he had allowed no hits during a 9⅔-inning relief stint, getting the win in a 17-inning game against the St. Louis Browns. In 1920, Ray helped the Indians to the American League pennant with a 20–10 record. He lost in his only World Series outing, bowing in the third game to the Brooklyn Dodgers, 2–1, after he lasted only two-thirds of an inning.

Caldwell was one of 17 pitchers permitted to continue throwing the spitball after it was outlawed in 1920. Owner of superb control, he was a fine fielder (on occasion he played center field for the Yankees). Also an excellent base runner and hitter, he ranks third in stolen bases and fourth in pinch hits on the all-time list for pitchers. He once hit a home run on three successive days, the first two as a pinch-hitter.

The talented Caldwell is one of many outstanding players (along with those mentioned elsewhere) who graduated to high levels of prominence in the major leagues from Philadelphia's surrounding counties and nearby areas in South Jersey and Delaware, and who played primarily for teams other than those from Philadelphia.

Another top Philadelphia suburbanite is catcher Mike Scioscia. Born in Upper Darby and raised in Morton, Scioscia went from Springfield (Delaware County) High School to the big leagues, where he became one of the top catchers of his era during a 13-year career that reached from 1980 to 1992.

Scioscia played entirely with the Los Angeles Dodgers. Although he was a member of the San Diego Padres and Texas Rangers at the end of his career, he did not play with those clubs because of injuries. A first-round pick (19th overall) in the 1976 draft, Scioscia was a two-time All-Star Game selection and is the Dodgers' all-time leader in games caught with 1,395.

The sturdy backstop, who was known for his rocklike blocks of home plate, was a key member of Dodgers teams that won National League pennants and World Series in 1981 and 1988. He finished his career with a .259 batting average with 68 home runs and 446 RBI. His career fielding percentage was a remarkable .988. Ironically, Scioscia was succeeded in LA by another Philadelphia suburbanite, Mike Piazza.

Good lefthanded pitchers are another of the Philadelphia area's quality contributions to the big leagues. A fine southpaw was Jon Matlack, a hard-throwing hurler who came out of West Chester to spend 13 seasons in the big leagues. Matlack was the National League's Rookie of the Year in 1972 when he nailed down a 15–10 record with a 2.32 ERA. That season, he surrendered the 3,000th and final hit to the Pittsburgh Pirates' ill-fated star, Roberto Clemente.

Jon Matlack

He had a career 125–126 record with a 3.18 ERA in 361 games between 1971 and 1983. His best work came with the New York Mets, with whom he won in double figures five years in a row, including a 17–10 mark in 1976.

The West Chester High alumnus led the National League in shutouts twice. With Tom Seaver and Jerry Koosman, he was a key part of a deluxe threesome that pitched the Mets to the National League pennant in 1973. Matlack beat the Cincinnati Reds with a two-hitter (both hits by Andy Kosco) in the League Championship Series, but had no decisions in the World Series against the Oakland Athletics, although he made three starts, including the first and final games. He was also co-MVP (with Bill Madlock) in the 1975 All-Star Game when he got the win with a two-hit, four-strikeout, two-inning stint in a 6–3 National League victory.

John Smiley added his name to the list of prominent local lefties. Born in Phoenixville, Smiley compiled a 126–103 record during a career that stretched from 1986 through 1997. Hurling primarily

John Smiley

for the Pittsburgh Pirates and Reds, the tall, hard-throwing graduate of Perkiomen High won in double figures seven times while—just like Matlack—pitching in 361 games. John's best year came in 1991 when he posted a 20–8 record with the Pirates, winners of the NL East division championship. That year, Smiley tied for the league lead in both wins and winning percentage (.714) and ranked third in the circuit's voting for the Cy Young Award.

The name Edgar Smith may not be a household word, even in the Philadelphia area, but it belongs to yet another noteworthy lefthander from the region. A native of Columbus, New Jersey, near Burlington, Smith didn't have a dazzling record (73–113 during 10 years in the big leagues), but he was firmly attached to baseball history.

While hurling for the Chicago White Sox, the sly southpaw, aided by Ted Williams's three-run homer in the bottom of the ninth inning, was the winning pitcher in the American League's 7–5 triumph in the 1941 All-Star Game. Smith, who broke in with the Philadelphia Athletics in 1936, tossed a two-hitter but lost, 1–0, in 1940 when Cleveland's Bob Feller hurled the only no-hitter ever pitched on opening day. He also served up Joe DiMaggio's first hit at the start of his 56-game hitting streak in 1941, as well as hits by the Yankee slugger in the 19th and 55th games of his streak. Once, Smith struck out New York's Lou Gehrig, DiMaggio, and Bill Dickey on 10 pitches.

One of Chester's many contributions to the major leagues was Lew Krausse, Jr. In 1961 when he signed a pro contract for a reported $125,000—after pitching three straight no-hitters during his senior year at Chester High—young Lew was baseball's biggest bonus baby. Going straight to the big leagues, as a major league rule then mandated, Krausse hurled a three-hit shutout to win his first game for the Kansas City A's, 4–0, over the California Angels.

A few years later, while pitching in the Venezuelan Winter League, Krausse struck out 33 in two games, one being a 21-strikeout one-hitter in which he fanned 10 straight batters. Lew also

Lew Krausse, Jr.

toiled for the Oakland A's, Milwaukee Brewers, Red Sox, St. Louis Cardinals, and Atlanta Braves, compiling a 68–91 record with a 4.00 ERA in 321 games spread out over 12 seasons.

Another suburban contribution to the majors was righthanded pitcher Lew Richie. He came out of Ambler to make good in the majors. During an eight-year career that ran from 1906 through 1913, the 5-foot, 8-inch hurler registered a 74–65 record with a 2.54 ERA while playing in 241 games with the Philadelphia Phillies, Boston Braves, and Chicago Cubs, the team for which he did his best work. Richie went 15–11 and 16–8 in back-to-back campaigns with the Cubs in 1911 and 1912.

Another player from that era was Steve Yerkes of Hatboro. An infielder, Yerkes played in seven seasons between 1909 and 1916, most of it with the Red Sox. He spent nearly four years as a Boston regular, playing both second base and shortstop. Yerkes also played in the Federal League before ending his career with a .268 batting average.

South Jersey sent its share of players to the big leagues. One of particular note was William (Wid) Conroy of Camden. He played in 11 seasons between 1901 and 1911, performing originally as a shortstop and later at third base. Conroy also put in time in the outfield.

He was the starting shortstop with the Milwaukee Brewers in the National League in 1901. Conroy played with the National League's pennant-winning Pirates in 1902 before jumping to the infant American League, where he was the first third baseman on the newly formed Highlanders (later renamed the Yankees) in 1903. Wid played in the Highlanders' first game and batted sixth. In six seasons with the Highlanders, he led the team in various categories, and he is currently tied for fifth on the Yankees' all-time stolen base list.

Known for his broad knowledge of baseball, Conroy finished his career with the Washington Senators. In his final season Conroy set

Wid Conroy

a still-standing American League record for third basemen with 13 assists in one game. He hit .248 in 1,374 games, his career high coming in 1905 when he hit .273 for the Highlanders. Later, he was a coach with the Phillies in 1922 and long-time minor league manager.

Then there was Danny Green. An outfielder from Burlington, he spent eight years in Chicago, four with the Cubs and four with the White Sox. He was a starter during six of those years. Green, who broke into the majors in 1898 before stepping out after the 1905 season, hit .293 in 923 games. A top base stealer, he hit above .290 six times, including .313 in 1901 and .312 in 1902 when he jumped to the American League.

Two fine relievers also came out of South Jersey. Fireballing Rawley Eastwick went from Camden and Haddonfield High School to an eight-year big league career. His best work was with Cincinnati. In 1975 and 1976 he led the National League in saves with 22 and 26, respectively, while helping the Big Red Machine to two pennants and two World Series victories. Considered one of the best relievers of the mid-1970s, Eastwick, who toiled with the Phillies in 1978 and 1979, finished with a 28–27 record and 68 saves. He rates a place in baseball history as the pitcher who gave up Hank Aaron's last National League home run (number 733) in 1974.

Born in Beverly, Barney Schultz from Burlington High School knuckleballed his way to a 20–20 record with 35 saves during seven big league seasons. In 1962 he tied a record by relieving in nine games in a row. His most notable work came in 1964 with the Cardinals. That year, Schultz worked in seven of the Cards' last nine games, and his 14 saves and 1.64 ERA helped the club come from behind to win the National League pennant.

Another South Jerseyite who also hailed from Camden was pitcher Fred Heimach, who toiled for 13 seasons between 1920 and 1933. A lefthander, Heimach divided his time between starting and relieving while playing his first six-plus seasons with the Athletics, then with the Red Sox and Yankees before going his last four years with the Brooklyn Dodgers. A career 62–69 record in 296 games was highlighted by marks of 14–12 with the 1924 A's and 11–6 with the 1929 Yankees.

A top player from Delaware was New Castle's Dave May, a 12-year veteran between 1967 and 1978. While playing with five big league teams, the outfielder registered a career batting average of .251 with 96 home runs and 422 RBI. May hit .303 in 1973 with the Brewers, getting career highs in home runs (25) and RBI (93) that year and hitting in 24 straight games. One year later, the Brewers traded May and a minor leaguer to the Atlanta Braves for none other than a guy named Hank Aaron.

John (Hans) Lobert emerged from Wilmington to spend 14 years in the majors during seasons that ranged from 1903 to 1917. Regarded at the time as the fastest man in the National League,

Dave May

Hans once stole second, third, and home. He also raced a horse around the infield, leading briefly but losing in the backstretch. Primarily a third baseman, Lobert had a lifetime average of .274 while playing mostly with the Reds, Phillies, and New York Giants. He hit over .300 four times, his best mark coming in 1912 when he punched out a .327 average with the Phillies.

It should be mentioned that a group of prominent players who performed essentially in other cities and who were born outside of the Philadelphia area spent much of their time growing up in the region. Among them are these:

Lewis (Hack) Wilson lived between the ages of six and 17 in Leiperville (Delaware County), although he was born in Ellwood City,

Hans Lobert

Pennsylvania. Hack, an outfielder, had a relatively short, 11-year career, but his .307 career batting average, 244 home runs, and 1,062 RBI were more than enough to get him elected to the Hall of Fame in 1979. Wilson led the National League in home runs four times and in RBI twice. His 190 RBI in 1930 are still an all-time record. That year, playing with the Cubs, Hack hit .356 with 56 home runs. Wilson spent six years with the Cubs and ended his career with the Phillies in 1934.

Orel Hershiser, although born in Buffalo, New York, lived for a number of years in Cherry Hill, New Jersey, where he graduated from Cherry Hill East High School. A fine major league pitcher, Hershiser had a 204–150 record in an 18-year career, most of it spent with the Los Angeles Dodgers. The Cy Young Award winner and the National League Pitcher of the Year in 1988 when he posted a 23–8 mark, Hershiser played in three All-Star Games and three World Series (3–3). He was the Most Valuable Player in the 1988 LCS with the Dodgers and the 1995 LCS with Cleveland, and the World Series MVP in 1988 when he hurled two complete-game victories—one being a shutout—in LA's triumph in five games over Oakland.

Another excellent pitcher was Len Barker, a native of Fort Knox, Kentucky, but a long-time resident of Langhorne and graduate of Neshaminy High School. While pitching with the Indians in 1981, Barker became one of just 15 hurlers who fired a perfect game in the 20th century, blanking the Toronto Blue Jays, 3–0. He compiled a 74–76 record in 11 years of service, his best year coming in 1980 when he went 19–12.

Phoenixville High School alumnus Andre Thornton put in 14 years in the majors after originally being signed by the Phillies. The native of Tuskegee, Alabama, was a .254 lifetime hitter with 253 home runs, accumulated mostly with the Indians. Thornton, primarily a first baseman, hit .293 in 1975 and .281 in 1983, and three times hit more than 30 home runs. He drove in 116 runs in 1982 and 105 in 1978. Thornton was the winner of the 1979 Roberto Clemente Award, which goes annually to the major league player who has best exemplified baseball on and off the field

Among others, Howie Bedell came out of Pottstown to play the outfield for parts of two years in the majors. Bedell, whose birthplace was Clearfield, Pennsylvania, collected his only RBI with the Phillies when he drove in the run in 1968 that broke the 58⅔-inning scoreless streak of the Dodgers' Don Drysdale.

Bob Sebra, a graduate of Gloucester Catholic High School and native of Ridgewood, New Jersey, pitched with four teams (including the Phillies) during parts of four big league seasons in the 1980s, posting a 15–29 record.

Outfielder Earl Rapp, a three-year veteran who hit .262 with five American League teams between 1949 and 1952, was born in

Corunna, Michigan, but grew up in the Salem, New Jersey, area and attended the old Swedesboro High School. His biggest year came as a minor leaguer when he drove in 145 runs and hit .347 in 181 games with the Pacific Coast League champion Oakland Oaks. Rapp also collected 133 RBI in 1955 with the PCL's San Diego Padres.

City Guys Who Got Away

Players Who Left Town to Perform Elsewhere

Among the Philadelphia area's many talented players, none was probably any more exciting than Pat Kelly. Not only was he a fine hitter, but he had exceptional speed as well. The combination of the two made Kelly well worth the price of admission for fans who watched him during his 15-year career in the major leagues.

Kelly came by his talent naturally. His older brother was Leroy Kelly, Hall of Fame running back of the Cleveland Browns. Pat himself was a fine football player as a highly mobile quarterback at Simon Gratz High School, where he also starred in basketball.

A slender lefthanded outfielder, Kelly briefly attended Morgan State College before getting signed by the Minnesota Twins in 1962. Subsequently, he played with the Kansas City Royals, Chicago White Sox, Baltimore Orioles, and Cleveland Indians before retiring after the 1981 season.

Pat Kelly

In his prime, Kelly was one of the American League's top base stealers. He pilfered 40 bases in 1969 and 34 the following year. His career total was 250.

To steal a base, you first have to get on base, and Kelly was no slouch in that category either. He hit .280 or above four times, his high coming in 1971 when he hit .291 while playing his first of six years with the White Sox. His career batting average was .264 with 1,147 hits and 76 home runs. Kelly was also a fine defensive player, only once making more than six errors in a season.

Kelly was a member of one All-Star team (1979). He also played with the American League champion Orioles in 1979. His home run, single, and three RBI helped the Orioles clinch the pennant in a four-game League Championship Series with the California Angels.

Many other players emerged from Philadelphia to carve out successful careers in the big leagues mostly with teams outside of the area. One was pitcher Mark Gubicza.

Mark Gubicza

A standout hurler and native of Roxborough, Gubicza came from a long line of outstanding pitchers who toed the mound at Penn Charter. From 1984 through 1997 during a 14-year career spent almost entirely with Kansas City, the rangy righthander fashioned a 132–136 record in 384 games.

A second-round draft choice in 1981, Gubicza won 84 games in his first six years in the big leagues, topping the spurt with a 20–8 record in 1988. He was third in the American League Cy Young Award voting that year.

Before he was slowed by injuries, Gubicza, a workhorse who started more than 30 games in a season four times and who won in double figures seven times, was considered one of his league's best hurlers. A two-time All-Star and owner of a one-hitter thrown in 1995 against the Oakland Athletics, the 6-foot, 6-inch Gubicza ranks among the all-time leaders on most of the Royals pitching records.

Like Roxborough, Frankford was also one of the city's baseball hotbeds. One of the most prominent members of its baseball populace was righthanded pitcher Bill Dietrich, an outstanding running back and captain of the football team at Frankford High School and also a star schoolboy basketball player.

Dietrich, a high school sensation in baseball who averaged 16 strikeouts per game in his senior year, was one of three big league pitchers from the Philadelphia area who fired a major league no-hitter (the others are Bill McCahan and Ray Caldwell). Dietrich's was an 8–0 whitewash of the St. Louis Browns in 1937.

Also the owner of a minor league perfect game thrown as a 20-year-old for Harrisburg in 1930, the fireballing Dietrich, one of baseball's few bespectacled players of his era, was originally signed by the Philadelphia Athletics. After making the majors with the A's in 1933, he pitched briefly with the Washington Senators before joining the White Sox in 1936.

Over the next 10 years, Dietrich—nicknamed "Bullfrog"—was one of the Chisox' top hurlers, his best season coming in 1944 when he posted a 16–17 record in a career-high 246 innings for a seventh-place team. He also lost two other no-hit bids in the ninth inning, one when Hank Greenberg of the Detroit Tigers singled with two outs. With age and elbow problems slowing him down, Dietrich concluded his career back with the A's in 1948, finishing his 16-year stint with a 108–128 record in 366 games.

Bill Dietrich

Righthanded pitchers were always one of Philadelphia's staples. Walt Masterson, another moundsman who wore glasses, was part of that contingent. Originally from West Philadelphia, he grew up in Juniata Park and attended North Catholic High School.

Although passed over by a number of scouts, Masterson was signed by Washington and went directly from high school to the big leagues. He made his debut in 1939 as an 18-year-old with a complete-game, 4–1 win over Bobo Newsom and the Tigers, striking out Greenberg with the bases loaded in the eighth inning to preserve the win.

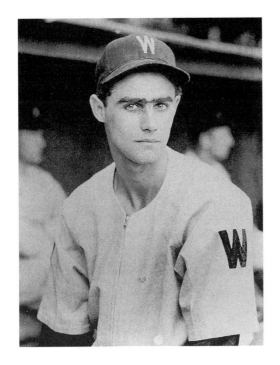

Walt Masterson

Sent to the minors to get some experience shortly afterward, Masterson soon returned, and except for three years of military service in World War II, spent until 1949 with the Senators. Working frequently in relief, he then pitched nearly three years with the Boston Red Sox before returning to Washington in 1952.

Hampered by control problems through much of his career, the hard-throwing Masterson won in double figures three times, his highest total coming in 1947 with 12 wins. That year, he pitched 16 scoreless innings in a game against the White Sox before leaving for a pinch-hitter in the 17th. Chicago won in the 18th, 1–0. Walt went on to hurl 34 consecutive scoreless innings. After going back to the minors where he spent three seasons, Masterson finished his career with the Senators in 1956, compiling a 78–100 record with 20 saves in 399 games.

When it comes to bizarre careers, few can top that of Harry (Socks) Seibold. Born in the Brewerytown section of the city, Seibold was originally a shortstop who made his major league debut with the Athletics in 1915. A weak hitter, Seibold was converted to pitcher, and by 1917 was a full-time hurler, despite a 4–16 record that year.

After going 7–20 over parts of three seasons as a pitcher with the A's—with one year out for military service—Seibold disappeared from the big leagues. For the next 10 years, he played either in the minors or in semipro leagues in Philadelphia. He finally resurfaced with the Boston Braves in 1929. Over a three-year period with the Braves, Seibold won 37 and lost 51 for a downtrodden Boston team that was buried deep in the National League's second division. His best year was in 1930 when he went 15–16. That year, while getting the win by a 5–1 count, Socks was the last major league batter to face Grover Cleveland Alexander, toiling then for the Phillies.

Noted as a control pitcher with a hot temper, Seibold claimed that his main pitch was "a five-cent curve." He finished his playing career in 1933 with a 48–85 record in 191 games. For a number of years thereafter, he managed in the minor leagues and later served as a scout for the Phillies.

Overbrook High School is noted for its great basketball players, but it also delivered a fine baseball player to the professional ranks. *The Sporting News* Rookie of the Year in 1979 and the Most Valuable Player in the 1987 League Championship Series, outfielder Jeff Leonard spent 14 productive seasons in the major leagues.

Signed originally by the Los Angeles Dodgers, Leonard spent five years in the club's farm system before getting traded to the Houston Astros. In his first full season he hit .290. Leonard was dealt to the San Francisco Giants in 1981 and spent all or parts of eight years with the California team. Later, he played with the Milwaukee Brewers and Seattle Mariners before retiring after the 1990 campaign.

Jeff Leonard

A member of the National League All-Star team in 1987—a year in which he hit .417 and drilled four home runs in a losing cause for the Giants in the LCS against the Cardinals—Leonard had his best year in 1984 when he hit .302 with 21 home runs and 86 RBI. He reached double figures in home runs five other times, finishing his career with 144 four-baggers to go along with a .266 batting average and 723 RBI.

Another city guy of recent vintage is South Philadelphian John Marzano, who came out of Central High School and Temple Uni-

John Marzano

versity to carve a 10-year career in the majors, mostly as a backup catcher. Marzano's career batting average was .241.

A first-team college All-American when he hit .409 as a senior and a member of the 1984 United States Olympic team, Marzano spent the better part of his career with the Red Sox, breaking into the big leagues in 1987 and playing six years in Boston before seeing service with the Texas Rangers and Mariners.

Left fielder Al Spangler was one of three graduates of Olney High School who made the majors (the others were Del Ennis and Lee Elia). In 13 seasons between 1959 and 1971, Spangler, who graduated as a mathematics major from Duke University, played with the Milwaukee Braves, Houston Colts/Astros, California Angels, and Chicago Cubs, batting .262 overall. Picked by the new Colts in the expansion draft, he was a regular with Houston from 1962 to 1964, hitting a career-high .285 in the team's first season. He followed that the next year with a .281 mark.

Philadelphia's other Pat Kelly, a veteran of nine years, including seven with the New York Yankees, was essentially a utility infielder. The one exception was in 1993 when he hit .273 as the Yankees' starting second baseman. Playing from 1991 to 1999, Kelly, who attended West Chester University, had a career .249 batting average, his high coming in 1994 when he hit .280.

Surprisingly, also born in Philadelphia but raised in California was infielder Brook Jacoby, an 11-year big league veteran who broke in with the Atlanta Braves in 1981 before performing as the regular third baseman with the Indians for nearly eight years. Jacoby, an American League All-Star in 1986, hit .300 with 32 home runs the following year. He finished his playing days with a .270 batting average with 120 home runs.

A contemporary of Jacoby's was Dion James, a Philadelphia outfielder who also relocated as a child to California. He played with four teams during an 11-year career that ran from 1983 to 1996. A .288 lifetime hitter, James had his best year in 1987 when he batted .312 as the regular center fielder with the Braves. James spent several seasons as a starter with the Braves and briefly with the Yankees.

Dion James

Going back a way, Ralph Young, another Philadelphian, performed for nearly nine years in the majors, breaking in with the Yankees in 1913, spending seven years with the Tigers, then finishing his career in 1922 with the Athletics. Young, a hustling second baseman, was a regular during six of his seasons with the Tigers and in his one year with the A's. He had back-to-back years of .291 and .299 in 1920 and 1921 before winding up his career with a .247 average.

Just before Young, Philadelphia infielder John Knight had a .239 career mark while playing between 1905 and 1913 with the Athletics, Red Sox, Yankees (Highlanders), and Senators. Although he played every infield position, Knight, a Central High School alumnus, performed primarily as a third baseman and shortstop, seeing regular duty with Boston in 1907 and with New York from 1909 to 1911. Nicknamed "Schoolboy," Knight led the Yankees in batting (.312) and in doubles (25) in 1910. The following year, he was paid a salary of $4,500, an extremely high figure for his era.

Another player from that era was outfielder Bill Hinchman, also a native of Philadelphia. Playing either left or right field, Hinchman began with the Cincinnati Reds in 1905. In 1907 he became a regular with the Indians, never hitting for a high average but starting for three straight years. Hinchman disappeared from the big leagues after the 1909 season. He re-emerged with the Pittsburgh Pirates in 1915 and was a regular for two seasons, hitting .307 and .315 and leading the National League in triples with 16 in 1916. Overall, Hinchman played in 10 big league seasons, ending his stint in the big time in 1920 with a career .261 batting average.

Catcher Al Spohrer was a big leaguer during eight seasons from 1928 to 1935. A .259 lifetime hitter with a .272 high in 1929, Spohrer played just two games with the New York Giants before getting swapped to the Braves. The Philadelphia lad was in Boston's starting lineup in six of his slightly more than seven years there.

The Current Contingent

Recent Major Leaguers from the Region

Doing a friend a favor is not normally something that is carried out with the hope of immediate reciprocation. But once in a great while there's a quick and unexpected payback.

Such was the case when Norristown native Tom Lasorda chose an obscure high school catcher named Mike Piazza for the Los Angeles Dodgers in the 62nd round (1,390th out of 1,433 players picked) of the 1988 draft. Lasorda, the boy's godfather, made the selection as a favor to the youngster's dad, Vince.

The Norristown-born Piazza had been a talented player at Phoenixville High School—he was named MVP of both his schoolboy and American Legion leagues. As a youth, he'd even received some hitting tips from the great Ted Williams in the batting cage set up at the Piazza's Valley Forge home. But a major league prospect? The big kid with the sunny disposition was merely drafted because one friend was doing something nice for another.

Or so it seemed. Little did anyone dare to imagine what the next 15 years would bring.

Today, no one lists the top catchers in baseball without mentioning Piazza. In a little more than 10 seasons in the major leagues while performing for the Dodgers, Florida Marlins, and New York Mets, he has recorded offensive numbers that are virtually unmatched by big league backstops of this or any era. When the time comes, it will not be possible to keep Piazza out of baseball's Hall of Fame.

Rookie of the Year in 1993, a 10-time All-Star selection, and the MVP of the 1996 game, Piazza had a career batting average of .321 through the 2002 season, having hit .300 or more nine times. Neither Bill Dickey, Mickey Cochrane, Roy Campanella, Yogi Berra, nor Johnny Bench—generally considered the five best-hitting catchers of all time—had career batting averages as high as Piazza's.

He has hit 24 or more home runs in each season, a major league record for catchers, and a career total of 347 through 2002. Only one player (Carlton Fisk with 351) has hit more career homers as a catcher than Piazza (335). And the rock-ribbed backstop has played in at least 140 games in a season five times.

Piazza, who has hit 35 or more home runs six times during a season, had his best year in 1997 while playing with the Dodgers. Not only did he club 40 homers for the first of two times in his career, but he also had a .362 batting average, collected 124 RBI, scored 104 runs, and slammed a career-high 201 hits while playing in 152 games. It was one of the greatest single-season performances by a catcher in big league history.

Mike grew up avidly following the Phillies, but he has shown no mercy for his hometown team. During his career, he has lashed 37 home runs and collected 108 RBI while blasting Phils pitching for a .337 average.

Piazza, who spent much of the 2003 season on the disabled list, leads an astonishingly large number of local players currently per-

Mike Piazza

forming in the major leagues. During the 2001, 2002, and 2003 seasons, 22 of them made big league appearances, including a few surprises. (Author's note: This book was published before the 2003 season concluded.)

Who, for instance, knew that star Cincinnati Reds first baseman Sean Casey was born locally? Originally drafted by the Cleveland Indians before getting traded to the Reds, the graduate of the University of Richmond, where he was second-team All-American, drew his first breath in Willingboro, New Jersey. A four-year veteran, Casey is a two-time All-Star with a .302 career batting average following the 2002 season, his best campaign coming in 1999 when he hit .322 with 25 home runs and 99 RBI.

Casey moved as a youngster to Upper St. Clair, Pennsylvania, where he was a high school teammate of infielder Kevin Orie, himself a native of West Chester. Orie was one of the National League's top rookies in 1997 when he was the regular third baseman for the Chicago Cubs and hit .275. Later, he played with the Marlins and in the Phillies farm system at Scranton/Wilkes-Barre, among other places, before returning to the Cubs in 2002, where he made a late-season appearance as a utility man.

Another big name in the current field is that of pitcher Jamie Moyer, a crafty lefthander who was born in Sellersville and attended Souderton High School, where he played baseball, basketball, and golf. Moyer attended St. Joseph's University and set a single-season school record there with 16 wins, 90 strikeouts, and a 1.99 ERA in 1984. His number 10 was the first baseball number retired at St. Joe's. Eventually, Moyer got his degree in 1996 from the University of Indiana.

Moyer is one of those guys who just keep getting better with age. As a 39-year-old during the 2001 season, he won 20 games for the Seattle Mariners, becoming the oldest pitcher in major league history to win 20 games for the first time. Jamie's mark of 20–6 led the rampaging Mariners to an American League record 116 wins during the regular season. Moyer's win total also tied him with Randy Johnson for the most Mariners victories by a pitcher in one season.

A veteran of more than 13 years in the majors, Moyer had a 92–44 record with Seattle from 1997 through 2002. His overall mark is 164–125, accumulated while playing with six major league teams, including his original team, the Cubs. Moyer has won in double figures nine times. He went 17–5 for Seattle in 1997.

Jamie Moyer

Philadelphia has made a noteworthy contribution to the current list of players in the person of Detroit Tigers outfielder Bobby Higginson. A graduate of Frankford High School, Higginson attended Temple University, where he hit .377 in three seasons and set the school's all-time home run record with 30.

A 12th-round pick of the Tigers in 1992 (after being an 18th-round choice of the Phillies the previous year), Bobby broke into the big leagues in 1995 and has been a regular member of Detroit's outfield ever since. A .281 lifetime hitter through 2002, his best years came in 1996 when he hit .320 and in 2000 when he hit .300 with career highs in home runs (30) and RBI (102).

Bobby Higginson

Joe McEwing

Infielder/outfielder Joe McEwing is also a prominent name on the local list. A graduate of Bishop Egan High School and a 28th-round draft choice of the St. Louis Cardinals in 1992 after attending County College of Morris in Randolph, New Jersey, the Bristol native broke into the majors late in 1998 with the Cardinals. Playing full-time the following year, he hit .275 and was sixth in the voting for National League Rookie of the Year. While playing primarily at second base but at every position except pitcher and catcher, he also had a 25-game hitting streak, a Cardinals rookie record and fifth-longest streak by a rookie in major league history.

Traded to the Mets after that season, McEwing has become a valuable utility man, performing in both the infield and outfield and serving as a pinch-hitter. Called "Super Joe," he played in left, center, and right fields, at third and second bases, and at shortstop. McEwing hit a big league high of .283 in 2001.

Catcher Ben Davis, born in Chester and a resident of Aston, came out of Malvern Prep, where he hit .507 in his senior year, to become the second player chosen in the 1995 draft. Picked by the San Diego Padres, Davis, whose brother Glenn was a first round choice of the Dodgers in 1997, had spent all or parts of five seasons in the majors through 2002. He cracked the starting lineup for the first time for the whole season in 2001, hitting .239 with the Padres. That year he became the center of a controversy when his eighth-inning bunt single snapped Curt Schilling's bid for a no-hitter. Traded to the Mariners during the off-season, Davis has caught more than one-half of Seattle's games since then.

Pitcher Scott Schoeneweis was in his fourth year on the mound with the Anaheim Angels in 2002, having posted a 27–30 career record by the end of that campaign. Originally a starter before he was switched to the bullpen during the 2002 season, Schoeneweis, who was traded to the Chicago White Sox during the 2003 season, was born at a hospital in Long Branch, New Jersey, but is a local guy who grew up in Mount Laurel and graduated from Lenape High

Mike Koplove

School. He is a graduate of Duke University, where he majored in history.

In the last year or two, a number of other players from the Philadelphia region have cracked the rosters of big league teams. One of them is Mike Koplove out of Chestnut Hill Academy and the University of Delaware. He first appeared during the 2001 season as a reliever for the Arizona Diamondbacks, and has been a key figure in the club's bullpen over the last two years. In 2002, he had a 6–1 record in 55 games.

Casey Fossum, who lived his first 12 years in Cherry Hill—even playing for a New Jersey state finalist Little League team—before moving to Texas, broke in with the Boston Red Sox in 2001, posting a 3–2 record in 13 games. A member of the team's starting rotation in 2003 before going on the disabled list, Fossum was a first-round pick out of Texas A & M in 1999 after leading the Aggies to the College World Series and twice being an All–Big 12 selection.

Two other young players from the area are Bishop Eustace High School graduates. Shortstop Mike Moriarity, an All–Big East selection at Seton Hall University, was born in Camden. He made his big league debut in 2002 with the Baltimore Orioles, then signed with the Toronto Blue Jays during the off season. Florida Marlins pitcher Blaine Neal, a 6-foot, 5-inch, 240-pound righthander who hails from Marlton, got his first taste of the majors in 2001 and was still in the club's bullpen in 2003.

Infielder Ramon Martinez, a native Philadelphian who spent his first two years in the

Casey Fossum

Ramon Martinez

city—living at Sixth and Allegheny—before moving to Puerto Rico, was with the San Francisco Giants off and on in every season between 1998 and 2002. In 2000, while hitting .302, he made just one error in 88 games as a shortstop and second baseman. He was the club's regular shortstop through much of 2001 before resuming a utility role the following year. He signed as a free agent with the Cubs for the 2003 season.

Two other catchers came out of Philadelphia to play recently in the majors. Jesse Levis, who calls Northeast High his alma mater, played with the Indians and the Milwaukee Brewers between 1992 and 2001, compiling a .255 batting average. Ironically, Levis played with both the American and National League Brewers. A backup catcher throughout his big league career, Levis joined his hometown Phillies organization in 2003. Kansas City Royals backup backstop Mike DiFelice was born in Philadelphia but moved to Tennessee as a youth. He was a .239 hitter during all or parts of seven seasons in the majors, including nearly four years with the Tampa Bay Devil Rays and two stints with the Cardinals.

Hurler Bob File, a graduate of Father Judge High School and Philadelphia College of Textiles and Sciences (now Philadelphia University), is a Philadelphia native who cracked the majors in 2001, posting a 5–3 record in 60 games with the Blue Jays.

The Wilmington area is represented by a strong current contingent, not the least of whom is catcher Chris Widger. Although he was born in Wilmington, Widger was raised in Pennsville, New Jersey, where he graduated from Pennsville High School. Originally, Chris entered the big leagues in 1995 with Seattle. In 1997 he joined the Montreal Expos, and he was the club's regular catcher in 1998 and 1999. He returned to Seattle in 2000, was out of the bigs the following year, then joined the New York Yankees during the 2002 season and played with the Cardinals in 2003. Widger hit a career-high .264 in 1999 with 14 home runs and 56 RBI.

Chris Widger

Another veteran born in Wilmington is infielder/outfielder John Mabry, who grew up in Maryland. He first made the big leagues in 1994 with the Cardinals. Since then he has played with Seattle, San Diego, Florida, the Phillies, and Oakland. In 2003 he signed with the Mariners. As a rookie, Mabry's .307 batting average was the highest for a Cardinals freshman first baseman since Johnny Mize hit .329 in 1936. Mabry, who received numerous votes for Rookie of the Year, followed that season with .297 and .284 marks. Mabry, who attended West Chester University, played in part of the 2002 season with the Phillies before he was swapped for Jeremy Giambi in a trade with the Athletics.

Wilmington-born Kevin Mench made his big league debut with the Texas Rangers in 2002 and hit .260 with 15 home runs and 60

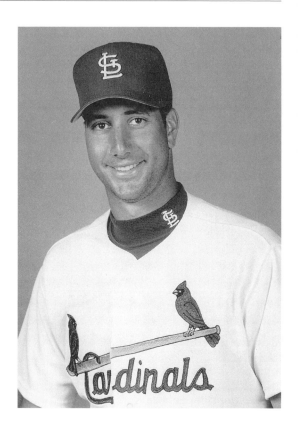

John Mabry

RBI. An outfielder, Mench was schooled at St. Marks High School and the University of Delaware, where he was twice named American East Conference Player of the Year.

Other Wilmington natives who made big league appearances in recent years include pitcher Wayne Franklin, who broke into the majors in 2000 with the Houston Astros, then moved to Milwaukee in 2002 and was in the Brewers' starting rotation in 2003. Two outfielders are Cliff Brumbaugh, who spent the 2001 season with the Texas Rangers and Colorado Rockies, and Pedro Swann, who cracked the big leagues for the first time in 2000 with the Atlanta Braves, then appeared with the Blue Jays in 2002.

6 Rarities, Oddities, and Ironies

The Status Quo Has Not Always Been Maintained

The true merit of any special gathering is not always measured by its quality or its quantity. Sometimes it helps to be unusual, too.

That's the case with some of the Philadelphia-area athletes who played baseball in the major leagues. Diverse and often rare characteristics are heavily represented among the group of native sons.

Some of these characteristics could be considered unique. Others could be classified as oddities. And a few might fall under the label of ironic. In any case, they add up to a fascinating collection of anecdotes that differ substantially from stature and statistics.

For instance, in 1923 the Boston Braves had a shortstop named Ernie Padgett. Ernie was a Philadelphia boy, a 5-foot, 8-inch 155 pounder who wound up playing five years in the big leagues, hitting .266 in 271 games.

On October 6 in the last game of the season, with Joe Batchelder pitching for the Braves, Padgett was playing in only his sec-

Ernie Padgett

ond major league game when he snared a line drive off the bat of Walter Holke. Padgett then touched second base to retire Cotton Tierney and tagged out Cliff Lee to complete an unassisted triple play.

Who do you think was the victim of Ernie's astonishing play? It was his hometown Philadelphia Phillies. And it was not only the first unassisted triple play in the National League since 1878, it was also the first of just five solo triple plays (the last one by the Phillies' Mickey Morandini) recorded by National Leaguers in the 20th century.

Incidentally, Padgett's heroics helped the Braves to a 4–1 victory in a game called after four and one-half innings because of darkness.

Remember when the Phillies captured the National League pennant in the last game of the 1950 season with a 4–1 victory over the Brooklyn Dodgers at Ebbets Field? Dick Sisler won the game with a three-run homer in the top of the 10th inning, and Robin Roberts got the win with a gritty complete game. But the game would've been over and Brooklyn would've tied for first place (requiring a special playoff) with a 2–1 win if it hadn't been for a great throw by Phillies center fielder Richie Ashburn that nailed Cal Abrams trying to score from second on Duke Snider's single to center. The throw is considered the greatest toss by a position player in Phillies history.

And what about the much-maligned Abrams, whom many Brooklynites loudly rebuked for not stopping at third (although he was sent home by Dodgers third base coach Milt Stock, ironically the Phillies' third baseman when they won their last pennant in 1915)? If Cal had stopped, the bases would've been loaded for the Dodgers with none out. Abrams, who had a respectable eight-year big league career while hitting .269, was of all things a native Philadelphian. He lived in the city until he was five years old before moving to Brooklyn where he grew up.

Cal Abrams

Here's another good one: Facing the Dodgers on October 4 in the fourth game of the 1947 World Series, Floyd (Bill) Bevens of the New York Yankees had a no-hitter and a 2–1 lead with two outs in the bottom of the ninth inning. It looked like it might be the fall classic's first no-hitter. But Bevens's dream of immortality came to a stunning end when Dodger pinch-hitter Cookie Lavagetto slammed a two-run double off the right-center-field wall to drive in two runs and give Brooklyn a 3–2 victory.

The winning run was scored by pinch-runner Eddie Miksis of Burlington, New Jersey. Lavagetto was batting for Eddie Stanky of Philadelphia.

Speaking of the Dodgers (both Brooklyn and Los Angeles varieties), the Philadelphia area played a major role in supplying the team with top-level catchers. During a 50-year period from the late 1940s to the late 1990s, the team's regular catcher during 29 of those years came from the region. Roy Campanella was the club's catcher for 10 years, Mike Scioscia for 13, and Mike Piazza for six.

The Philadelphia area also played an important role in the infamous Black Sox scandal of 1919 when eight members of the Chicago White Sox were charged with throwing the World Series to the Cincinnati Reds. Although cleared by a grand jury in Chicago, the eight were eventually suspended from baseball for life by commissioner Kenesaw Mountain Landis.

In keeping with its diversity, the Philadelphia area produced one of the alleged bribed players, the White Sox manager, one of the alleged fixers, and the son of one of the honest Chicago players.

Although he maintained his innocence throughout the rest of his life, Chicago's fine third baseman Buck Weaver, a Pottstown native, was accused of being one of the eight players who took money to throw the Series. Nevertheless, his splendid career was derailed after nine years in the majors. Manager Kid Gleason came from Camden. Billy Maharg, a small-time boxer who worked at a local Ford factory while consorting with the gamblers who fixed the Series, was a Philadelphian. And Eddie Collins, Jr., the son of the virtuous White Sox captain of the same name, called Lansdowne his birthplace.

Gleason was a baseball lifer who spent 22 seasons as a major league player, five as a manager, and 15 as a coach. Collins, a baseball star at Yale University, played in three seasons (1939, 1941–42) as a reserve outfielder with the Philadelphia Athletics, and later worked in the Phillies front office. And Maharg appeared in one game with the Detroit Tigers and one with the Phillies, although some claimed that he was really Peaches Graham (Maharg spelled backward), a reserve player who appeared in seven seasons between 1902 and 1912.

The one game in which Maharg appeared with the Tigers occurred in 1912 and was noteworthy because the team that day consisted entirely of Philadelphia players. This unusual situation was the result of a strike by Detroit's regular players, who were protesting the suspension of their star, Ty Cobb. Three days earlier in New York, Cobb had jumped into the stands to fight with a heckler, who it turned out was a crippled man.

Playing in Philadelphia against the Athletics, Detroit management, with the help of the A's Connie Mack, chose to field a makeshift team of local players masquerading as Tigers rather than get slapped with a heavy fine and a forfeit. Among the one-day big leaguers was Aloysius Travers, a St. Joseph's College student manager, who pitched for the only time in his life. He gave up 26 hits and 24 runs in a complete game outing that earned him $25. The 24–2 loss might have had something to do with Travers's decision to become a priest.

Lots of other odd things involving area residents happened over the years. Among them, two involved Philadelphians. When he was a coach with the Cincinnati Reds, Jimmie Wilson was called to duty as a substitute umpire when it turned out that no umpires had been assigned to a game with the St. Louis Cardinals. Athletics captain Harry Davis once argued so long about a play in which no interference was called after a base runner crashed into the A's shortstop that the beleaguered umpire forfeited the game to the New York Yankees. Phillies pitcher Dallas Green of Newport, Delaware, had the unpleasant distinction of tossing the ball that the New York Mets' Jimmy Piersall hit for his 100th home run, a feat that the outfielder celebrated—angering nearly everybody else—by running around the bases backward.

How's this for craziness? Jeff Leonard, then with the Houston Astros, once flew out twice and singled in the same at-bat. Uh?

With two outs in the ninth inning, Leonard flew out to center to seemingly end the game. But wait. Umpire Doug Harvey said that time had been called and ordered Leonard back to the plate. The Philadelphia native then singled. But that still wasn't the end of Leonard's trip to the dish. Umpires noticed that the opposing New York Mets had no first baseman. Back came Leonard to hit again. This time he flew out to left to end the game once and for all. By the way, the Mets won, 5–0.

Another one of the game's oddities had to do with a pitcher named Pete Cimino. Born in Philadelphia but raised in Bristol, Cimino twirled in four seasons in the big leagues in the late 1960s with the Minnesota Twins and California Angels. A reliever in all but one of his 86 games, Cimino had a 5–8 career record with a respectable 3.07 earned run average.

Pete Cimino

Cimino, however, had achieved more prominence as a basketball player. In 1959, while playing for Bristol High School in a game against Palisades (New Jersey) High, Cimino set a Pennsylvania state single-game scoring record with 110 points. Whose record did Cimino break? Just a guy named Wilt Chamberlain, who deposited 90 points for Overbrook High School in a 1955 game against Roxborough.

Some other Philadelphia-area baseball players had strong ties with basketball. Roxborough's Buddy Harris, a pitcher with the Houston Astros in the early 1970s, was the son of the long-time and highly successful head basketball coach at Philadelphia Textile, Bucky Harris.

Two brothers from Pottstown made high marks on the court before becoming professional baseball players. Dick Ricketts was a first team All-American hoopster at Duquesne in 1954–55, a season in which he scored 23 points to help the Iron Dukes to the NIT championship with a 70–58 win over Dayton (Si Green tallied 33 for the winners). Later, Dick pitched in 12 games (1–6 record) with the 1959 St. Louis Cardinals. Younger brother Dave, also a basketball star at Duquesne and a starter on the NIT winner, appeared in parts of six seasons between 1963 and 1970 with the Cardinals and Pittsburgh Pirates. A catcher, Dave hit .249 in 130 games. He later served for 16 years as a coach with the Cardinals.

Dave Ricketts

Basketball wasn't the only other sport that crossed paths with baseball for Philadelphia-area athletes. Pat Kelly, a three-sport star at Simon Gratz High, spent 15 years between 1967 and 1981 as a fine outfielder in the big leagues. His older brother was Leroy Kelly, a brilliant running back and six-time All-Pro during a 10-year career with the Cleveland Browns. A member of the Football Hall of Fame, Leroy twice led the NFL in rushing.

Ironically, there was another Pat Kelly born in Philadelphia who played big league baseball. This Pat, a second and third baseman, spent all or parts of nine years in the majors. He attended West Chester University after living as a teenager in Catasauqua, Pennsylvania.

Pat Kelly

Many other family relationships dot the roster of Philadelphia-area natives. Lew Krausse, Sr. and Jr., both born in Media, pitched in the big leagues. Amazingly, young Lew's first big league victory was a shutout and his father's last win was a whitewash. Lew, Sr., posted a 5–1 record in 23 games with the 1931–32 Athletics. Afterward, he managed in the minor leagues before serving for many years as a scout with the A's.

Another father-son combination that made the majors was pitchers Bill and Brett Laxton, each of whom graduated from Audubon High School. Bill, a Camden native who hurled in parts of five seasons in the 1970s after breaking in with the Phillies, had a 3–10 record with five teams. Brett, who came from Stratford, New Jersey, had an outstanding freshman season at Louisiana State University before signing with the Oakland Athletics for whom he made his big league debut in 1999, and was later traded for Jeremy Giambi to the Kansas City Royals. Ironically, Brett and another Philadelphia-area native, John Mabry of Wilmington, were each traded during their careers for Jeremy Giambi.

The Philadelphia area spawned some other players whose fathers (born elsewhere) had been major leaguers. The sons were all born there while their dads played with Philadelphia teams. The group includes outfielder Ruben Amaro (1991–98, Angels, Indians, Phillies), whose father Ruben, Sr., was an infielder; catcher Doug Camilli (1960–67, 1969, Los Angeles Dodgers, Washington Senators), son of first baseman Dolph; and outfielder Scott Northey (1969, Royals), son of outfielder Ron. All three were born in Philadelphia. Catcher Robbie Wine (1986–87, Houston Astros), son of shortstop Bobby, saw the first light of day in Norristown. Also, pitcher Ray Narleski's dad Bill played in the big leagues.

Several other sets of brothers made the majors. Pitcher Bobby Shantz and catcher Wilmer Shantz went from Pottstown to the bigs. The Ogden brothers, Johnny and Curly, both Swarthmore College alumni, reached the majors after pitching their way out of a town in Delaware County with the unlikely name of Ogden. Johnny, who posted a 216–94 record during a long career in the International League, later became a highly successful major league scout, signing among others Dick Allen for the Phillies and Bob Uecker for the Milwaukee Braves. Roy and Bill Thomas graced major league diamonds. So did Bill and Harry Hinchman and Joe and Patsy O'Rourke. And Kid Gleason's brother Harry went on to a brief stint in the big leagues, playing mostly as a third baseman before his career was essentially ended after he was beaned by Rube Waddell of the Athletics.

Another family combination was an uncle-nephew twosome. Philadelphia native Jack Meyer was a standout relief pitcher with the Phillies. His nephew Brian Meyer, born in Camden and raised in Medford Lakes, hurled in 34 games (0–5 record) as a reliever with the Astros from 1988 to 1990. Also noteworthy in the case of Jack Meyer is that he, Ruben Amaro, Jr., and Royals pitcher Mark Gubicza were all graduates of Penn Charter.

That group wasn't the only big league trio who graduated from the same Philadelphia-area high school. Incredibly, Eddie Miksis, Sam Calderone, and Barney Schultz were in the same class at Burlington High. Del Ennis, Lee Elia, and Al Spangler all went to Olney High. Tom Lasorda, Bobby Mitchell, and Roy Sherid were schooled at Norristown High. Joe Kerrigan, Bob File, and Joe Bontikowski list Father Judge as their alma mater. Eddie Stanky and Benny Culp graduated from the old Northeast High in the same class (1934).

The distinction for sending the most players to the big leagues, however, is held by Chester High. No less than seven Clippers wound up at the top of the heap: Danny Murtaugh, Lew Krausse, Jr., Ron Henry, Johnny Podgajny, Tom Chism, and the Ogden brothers. Five natives—the Shantz and the Ricketts brothers and Buck Weaver—attended Pottstown High, as did the transplanted Howie Bedell.

Seven players—Dick Koecher, Purn Goldy, Pete Filson, Kerrigan, John Marzano, Jeff Manto, and Bobby Higginson—attended Temple University. Manto spent 16 years in professional baseball, playing with eight major league teams, 15 minor league squads, and one club in Japan.

Pitcher Sigmund (Sig) Jakucki of Camden had an unusual big league résumé. He worked in the minors from 1934 to 1938 except for a brief (seven-game) appearance for the St. Louis Browns in 1936. He then left organized baseball, only to return in 1944 with the Browns. That season, the 35-year-old Jakucki had a 13–9 record and beat the Yankees, 5–2, in the final game of the

Jeff Manto

Sig Jakucki

Lena Blackburne

season to give the Browns their only pennant. Sig followed those heroics with a 12–10 mark in 1945, then vanished from the big leagues for good.

Another disappearing act was performed by Philadelphian Bill Haeffner, who for some unknown reason made appearances in the big leagues (for three different teams) in 1915, 1920, and 1928. And Clifton Heights native Lena Blackburne earned considerable prominence after a playing, coaching, managing, and scouting career as the man who supplied a special kind of mud that was rubbed onto all the baseballs used by the major leagues. (He always kept the source a secret, although the location was said to be Rancocas Creek near his home in Riverton, New Jersey.) Blackburne kept hundreds of coffee cans in which he stored the mud in his garage before selling it to the leagues for $14 per can.

The Philadelphia area also contributed a Tink and a Twink—Tink Turner from Swarthmore and Twink Twining from Horsham, each of whom pitched in just one major league game, for the Athletics and Cincinnati Reds, respectively. Philadelphian Bert Kuczynski, who appeared briefly with the Athletics in 1943, had been an All-American football player at the University of Pennsylvania.

Benny Culp, Dick Koecher, Frank Hoerst (from left)

And Frank Hoerst, whose five-year career as a Phillies pitcher was carved in two by World War II, was a standout basketball player (and later an assistant coach) at La Salle College in the late 1930s.

Many other players from the region acquired special footnotes to their names. In 1938, Philadelphia's Hal Kelleher gave up a club record 12 runs in one inning while hurling the Phillies to a 21–2 loss to the Chicago Cubs. Ken Reynolds of Trevose not only yielded the last hit (2,583) of Ernie Banks's career, but also tied a major league record in 1972 when he lost 12 straight games with the Phils.

The briefest Phillies pitching career came when in the last game of the 1928 season, Philadelphian Martin Van Buren (Marty) Walker gave up two hits and three walks in the first inning of his major league debut, and was yanked before retiring a batter. He never showed up in the big leagues again.

7 The Decision Makers

Managers of All Kinds Dictated Their Brands of Strategy

Seventeen natives of the Philadelphia area have managed major league baseball teams since 1900. Some of them strategized for lengthy periods, while others were strictly short-termers. Their rates of success varied from very good to not so good. And they came from many different backgrounds to fill their posts.

It does not take any special powers of the intellect to determine who was the best one. The winner by a comfortable margin is a skipper whose name in synonymous with winning. That name is Joe McCarthy.

McCarthy emerged from the Germantown section of Philadelphia to become not only the area's finest manager, but also one of the most successful pilots of all time. He was recognized for his achievements with induction into the Hall of Fame in 1957.

Marse Joe, as he was fondly called, has the highest managerial winning percentage in baseball history. His .615 mark was pro-

Joe McCarthy

duced from a 2,125–1,333 record during a 24-year career with the Chicago Cubs, New York Yankees, and Boston Red Sox. McCarthy's teams won nine pennants and seven World Series. He never had a second-division team, and his clubs finished below third place only four times. Twelve of his teams, including nine Yankees clubs, rank among the top 15 highest-scoring teams ever to take the field.

McCarthy's managerial philosophy was a simple one that could easily apply today. "A ballplayer has only two hours of concentrated work every day," he said. "If he can not attend to business with the high pay and the working conditions so pleasant, something is wrong with him and he ought to go somewhere else."

Some called McCarthy "a push-button manager," a reference to the obvious fact that all of his teams were well stocked with excellent players. Joe hated the description. So did his supporters, who always claimed that Marse Joe had a sharp mind that was as wise as it was clever. "McCarthy had an uncanny knack of knowing what was going on all over the field," Yankee star Tommy Henrich once said.

As a youth, McCarthy had played for a variety of local teams in the Philadelphia area before hooking on with a semipro team in Wilmington, Delaware. Eventually, he enrolled at Niagara University, but he dropped out after two years to become a minor league player. Joe was just an average player, his main distinction being that in 1914 while playing with Buffalo he became just the second batter to face a young kid pitcher named Babe Ruth (who fired a six-hit, 6–0 win that day for Baltimore). But after advancing to the Louisville Colonels, McCarthy became the club's playing-manager in 1919. Two years later he became a full-time pilot and won the minor league World Series.

McCarthy joined the Cubs in 1926. In 1929 he became the first manager to win a pennant without having played in the major leagues. Joe became Yankees skipper in 1932, and that year his club won 107 games and the American League pennant, making McCarthy the first manager to win flags in each league. The Yanks won the World Series that year, and they went on to win five more Series titles, including four in a row between 1936 and 1939, and six more pennants. Overall, six of those teams won more than 100 games.

Joe, now living on a farm near Buffalo, left the Yankees during the 1946 season. He took over the Red Sox in 1948, and that year led the team to a first-place tie before losing to the Cleveland Indians in a one-game playoff, the first in AL history. After a second-place finish in 1949, McCarthy left the Red Sox during the 1950 season, retiring to the farm.

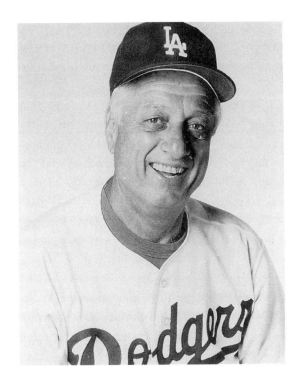

Tom Lasorda

McCarthy is one of two Hall of Fame managers from the Philadelphia area. The other is Tom Lasorda, who was inducted in 1997 after a glittering career as the skipper of the Los Angeles Dodgers.

With a 1,599–1,439 record spread over 21 seasons, Lasorda won four pennants and two World Series, those coming in 1981 and 1988. Overall, the peppy pilot's teams won seven division titles. Only three other pilots in the 20th century—Connie Mack, John McGraw, and Walter Alston—called the shots for one team longer than Tom.

Lasorda was baseball's winningest skipper in the 1980s. A perennial optimist who was as enthusiastic and animated as any pilot who ever set foot in a dugout, Tom took a special interest in the welfare of his players. For that reason, he—unlike many other managers—was especially popular with the men he directed. He was also a fixture among Hollywood celebrities and others with high public profiles.

Hollywood was a long way from Norristown where Lasorda grew up. A lefthanded pitcher, Lasorda was originally the property of the Philadelphia Phillies, the club with which he signed after graduating from Norristown High School in 1944. After two unspectacular years in the Phillies' farm chain, Tom was sold to the Brooklyn Dodgers. He bounced around the Dodgers' organization, once striking out 25 batters in a 15-inning game, until making his first big league appearance in 1954 in a game in which he threw three wild pitches in the same inning.

Tom pitched briefly with Brooklyn in 1954 and 1955, and with the Kansas City Athletics in 1956. In those three seasons, he appeared in 26 games, getting no wins in four decisions. After his short brush with the big leagues, Lasorda returned to the minor leagues with Montreal. By the time he finally packed it in as a player in 1961, he had won 107 International League games.

Lasorda spent the next four years as a scout with the Dodgers, then toiled for eight more years as a manager in the club's farm system, winning five pennants. Four more years were spent as the parent team's third base coach before the gregarious ex-pitcher was named manager of the Dodgers, succeeding Walter Alston early in the 1976 season. Lasorda promptly won pennants in his first two full years at the helm.

Long before he retired after the 1996 season, Lasorda was described as someone who "bled Dodger blue." Always a highly vocal goodwill ambassador for baseball, Lasorda capped his managerial career by leading the United States team to an Olympic gold medal in 2000.

Another Philadelphia-area manager who was particularly successful was Danny Murtaugh. Amazingly, over a period of 20 years,

Danny Murtaugh

Murtaugh put in four different terms in 15 seasons as skipper of the Pittsburgh Pirates. His overall record was 1,115–950 with two pennants, two World Series victories, and four division titles. He was named National League Manager of the Year three times.

Murtaugh was the manager when Bill Mazeroski hit one of baseball's most memorable home runs in the bottom of the ninth inning to give the Pirates a victory over the New York Yankees in the seventh game of the 1960 World Series. Danny also led the Bucs to a Series triumph in 1971 when Pittsburgh downed the Baltimore Orioles in seven games.

A highly respected, tough, but humorous Irishman, Murtaugh put in eight years during his first stint that went from 1957 through

1964, taking over a downtrodden team and turning it into an annual pennant contender in the National League. He returned for part of the 1967 season, then was called on again for the 1970 and 1971 seasons. Danny's last stint went from 1973 through 1976. Each time he was summoned to return, it was to bail out the Pirates from a difficult situation. Despite failing health, Murtaugh never complained, always loyally accepting the call of his long-time employer.

A peppery second baseman during nine big league seasons spent with the Phillies, Boston Braves, and Pirates, the Chesterborn Murtaugh began his career on the sidelines in 1952.

Collectively, McCarthy, Lasorda, and Murtaugh won 15 pennants and 11 World Series. While the three rank well above the others in terms of their respective managerial successes, two other local skippers have won World Series. The most recent is Mike Scioscia of the Anaheim Angels.

Mike Scioscia

A native of Morton and a graduate of Springfield (Delaware County) High School, the unflappable Scioscia led the Angels to victory in the 2002 World Series in his third year as skipper of the team. A wild-card entry, the Angels won the first American League pennant in the team's 42-year history after beating the New York Yankees and Minnesota Twins in the playoffs.

The Series victory in seven games over the San Francisco Giants culminated a year in which the Angels won 99 games after finishing 41 games out of first place the previous year. In 2002 the Angels ranked just 15th in the major leagues in total payroll. Scioscia, who played under Lasorda with Los Angeles Dodgers teams that won World Series in 1981 and 1988, was an easy winner in the balloting for American League Manager of the Year.

The only World Series winner in Phillies history was piloted by Dallas Green of Newport, Delaware. Green guided the 1980 Phils to victory in six games against the Kansas City Royals after the club had won a stunning League Championship Series in five games with the Houston Astros. For Green, a one-time student at the University of Delaware who skippered the Phillies from late 1979 through 1981 (169–130 record), it would be the highlight of his managerial career. Subsequent stints with the New York Yankees and Mets proved to be far less successful.

Jimmy Dykes, a Philadelphia native, performed with special distinction during 22 years as a player. He then managed six different teams during a career as a pilot that covered 21 seasons between 1934 and 1961. No other big league manager held the reigns of more teams, and only one other skipper (Clark Griffith) played in at least 20 seasons and managed in 20 or more campaigns during his major league career. In his travels, Dykes compiled a 1,406–1,541 overall record with the Chicago White Sox, Philadelphia Athletics, Baltimore Orioles, Cincinnati Reds, Detroit Tigers, and Cleveland Indians. His longest stint was 13 years with the White Sox, whom he took over as a player-manager. Dykes's Chicago club finished in third place three times, his highest finishes as a manager. In 1942, as manager of the Chisox, Dykes showed no interest in Jackie Robinson after giving him a brief tryout in spring training.

Although most of the teams that he managed were far from being contenders, Jimmy was the handpicked successor of Connie Mack in 1951 after the aging leader of the Athletics finally decided to step down. After three uneventful years in Philadelphia, Dykes

Dallas Green

in 1954 became the first manager of the Orioles after the team gave up the ghost as the St. Louis Browns.

One of the most memorable events in Dykes's career occurred in 1960 when he was traded for another manager, the only time in baseball history that one skipper has been swapped for another. In an apparent attempt to generate fan interest in their highly mediocre clubs, Detroit general manager Frank (Trader) Lane conspired with Cleveland GM Bill DeWitt to trade Dykes for Joe Gordon. Neither improved his team's place in the standings. When Dykes joined the Indians at the age of 64, he became one of the oldest managers ever hired.

Another manager who deserves mention is Philadelphian Jimmie Wilson, a catcher who in 1934 became one of many playing managers in the 1930s when he took over the Phillies. After guiding the Phils for five years, Wilson moved on to the Chicago Cubs, whom he directed for four more years. In nine years, while for the most part piloting terrible teams, Wilson's clubs finished eighth

Jimmie Wilson

three times and seventh three times. His overall record of 493–735 is noteworthy only because at .401, Wilson's percentage ranks as the lowest in baseball history for anyone who managed more than 1,000 games.

Much more successful was Philadelphia's Eddie Stanky, owner of a 467–435 career record while at the helm of the St. Louis Cardinals, White Sox, and Texas Rangers. Stanky pulled the strings for eight years, starting with the Cardinals in 1952 as yet another player-manager. St. Louis finished third that year, then tied for third the following year, Eddie's highest finishes. He had two other first-division finishes, winding up fourth with Chicago in both 1966 and 1967. Stanky, who served as the long-time coach of the baseball team at the University of South Alabama, was called back to the majors in 1977 to lead the Rangers, but he quit after one game, saying he had made a mistake returning to the big leagues.

William (Kid) Gleason came out of Camden to have a fine career as a player. As a manager, it was a different story. Gleason was the pilot of the infamous White Sox, who—known as the Black Sox—dumped the 1919 World Series. The White Sox that year were an outstanding team, running off with the American League pennant with an 88–52 record. In 1920, the year the scandal was exposed, Chicago posted a 96–58 mark, good for second place. But, following the expulsion of eight players, Gleason's three remaining seasons with the White Sox were sad, forlorn years from which the little skipper never quite recovered. He finished his five-year managerial career with a 392–364 record.

Philadelphia native Bill Shettsline was another manager with a different kind of résumé. Shettsline began his career with the Phillies as a handyman, then became a ticket taker. He rose through the ranks to become the team's manager in 1898. He then managed for four more years, finishing in second place once and third twice before ending his tenure in 1902 with a 367–303 overall record. Shettsline, who was a member of that rare species of manager who

Lee Elia

never played professionally, eventually became president of the Phillies.

Of the other managers from the Philadelphia area, none served in the driver's seat for very long. Philadelphia's Lee Elia worked for parts of two years with the Cubs (1982 and 1983) and two more years with the Phillies (1987 and 1988), going 238–300, with no team finishing higher than fifth. Mickey Vernon was the first manager of the expansion Washington Senators, and the two-time batting champion from Marcus Hook went 135–227 in two and one-half years from 1961 to 1963. In the late 1920s, Lena Blackburne of

Clifton Heights worked in parts of two years with weak White Sox teams, registering a 99–133 mark. Philadelphia native Bucky Walters put in less than two seasons with the 1948 and 1949 Reds while recording a log of 81–123. Harry Davis, also a Philadelphian, did one season with Cleveland in 1912, leaving before the end of the campaign with a 54–71 record. Hans Lobert of Wilmington guided two Phillies teams as an interim manager in 1938 and 1942, his chief claim to fame being that he unsuccessfully tried to get the club to change its name to Phils in what he thought was an attempt to erase the image of a loser that the name Phillies suggested.

Along with Scioscia, only one other area native has managed so far in the major leagues in the 21st century. Philadelphian Joe Kerrigan, the 2003 pitching coach of the Phillies, worked a partial season in 2001 with the Boston Red Sox.

8 Long, Long Ago

Noteworthy Players from the 19th Century

It would not be an exaggeration to say that Philadelphia and its suburbs have played as important a part in baseball history as any other region in the country. And that claim is not just a reference to the Philadelphia area's stature as a leading birthplace of major league players.

Indeed, baseball was played in Philadelphia as far back as the 1830s—even before Abner Doubleday was incorrectly believed to have invented the game. The area was credited as having been the location of numerous "firsts" in baseball. It has been claimed that the first batting title, the first unassisted triple play, and the first pinch-hit home run, as well as the first sliding pads and the first catcher's mask, all involved Philadelphia natives.

Philadelphia also gave birth to the first home run slugger.

His name was Harry Stovey, an outfielder/first baseman who had changed his name from Stowe to keep his mother from learning that he was a baseball player. At a time when home runs were as

Harry Stovey

uncommon as players without handlebar mustaches, Stovey showed that the heavy, almost comatose contrivance that was called a baseball could be swatted far enough out of the reach of fielders that a batter could circle the bases.

Stovey led his league in home runs five times, once hitting an astounding 19 homers in a single season (1889). He also led his league in extra base hits five times, in runs and triples each four times, and in slugging percentage three times.

The righthanded slugger from the Richmond section of Philadelphia played in 14 big league seasons, starting in 1880 with the Worcester Brown Stockings of the National League. Three years later he switched to his hometown Athletics (no relation to future Athletics teams) of the young American Association. Stovey put in seven seasons with the Athletics before moving on to Boston (both Players and National Leagues), Baltimore, and Brooklyn, where he finished his career in 1893 with a lifetime batting average of .289. The first major league player to reach 100 career home runs, Stovey clubbed the extraordinary total of 122 homers while driving in 908 runs.

Harry also tried his hand at managing. He piloted the Athletics in 1885 (55–57–1), after having been briefly at the helm of the Worcester Brown Stockings in 1881 (8–18–1).

Stovey's best season came in 1889 when he hit .308 and led the AA with 19 home runs, 119 RBI, 152 runs, and a slugging average of .525. He hit .326 in 1884 with 83 RBI and a league-leading 23 triples and 124 runs. It was the first time in the major leagues that a batter hit more than 20 triples in a season.

Harry, who went 5-for-5 five different times and twice hit three triples in one game, was not only a redoubtable hitter, he was also the best base runner of his era, and he twice led leagues in stolen bases. Over a six-year period between 1886 and 1891 he averaged 74 steals a season, once reaching a total of 97. Stovey once singled, stole second and third, and scored on a wild pitch to give the Athletics a 1–0 victory in a game that clinched the 1883 AA pennant by one game over Louisville. He is one of only two players in the 19th century (the other is Ed Delahanty) to win both home run and stolen base titles.

Stovey was credited with originating the feet-first slide and sliding pads to protect his often-bruised hips and legs. Opposing players laughed at him, but he wore them—the pads tied around his waist—anyway. Harry was also a master of the pop-up slide. "He looked like a jackknife that had just closed and opened again," someone said.

Although Stovey was the premier home run hitter of the 19th century, another Philadelphian who made a name for himself in that era was Ned Williamson. Playing mostly with the National League's Chicago White Stockings, who won five pennants while he was there, Williamson was a fine-fielding third baseman, and later a shortstop, with a strong throwing arm. He led the National League in fielding average five times before his career as a top player was essentially ended in 1889 when he damaged a knee sliding on a cinder infield. Five years later he died of consumption at the age of 36.

His most conspicuous feat in hitting a baseball occurred in 1884. He led the National League with 27 home runs, a major league mark that stood until Babe Ruth broke it 35 years later. The home runs, however, were to say the least tainted. The right-field fence at Chicago's Lakefront Park, where Williamson played, was a mere

180 feet from home plate. Although a righthanded batter, Ned easily popped balls—which had previously been ruled doubles—over the short barrier. He hit 25 of his 27 four-baggers there.

Williamson never hit higher than nine homers in any other season, finishing his 13-year career with 64. He was, however, the first major leaguer to homer three times in one game when he did it in 1884. While playing 11 years with the White Stockings, the genial and extremely popular player had a career batting average of .255. He led the league in doubles with 49 in 1883 when a ball hit over the short fence was still considered a ground-rule two-base hit.

In addition to Stovey and Williamson, the Philadelphia area produced many other outstanding baseball players during the 19th century. Not all of them are cited here, but some of the more noteworthy ones need to be mentioned in a book of this kind. (Note that in the 19th century five different leagues, playing at various times, were considered major leagues—the National Association, the National League, the American Association, the Union Association, and the Players or Brotherhood League.)

Jack Clements

One of the area's finest players was Jack Clements of Philadelphia. Incredibly, Clements was a left-handed catcher, something that is virtually nonexistent in baseball. For that reason, Clements caught more games than any other left-hander in baseball history (1,073, which is more than 800 above the next highest total).

The veteran of 17 seasons, however, was no ordinary catcher. He was one of the first backstops to wear a chest protector—a practice that drew jeers and catcalls from fans and opposing players. And he was a fine hitter who had a .286 lifetime batting average with 77 home runs.

Clements played a little more than 13 years with the Philadelphia Phillies, joining the club in 1884 after a brief sojourn in the short-lived Union Association with the Philadelphia Keystones. During his years with the Phillies, the unorthodox and colorful Clements became the first major league catcher ever to go behind the plate in 1,000 games. He also posted batting averages of .315, .310, .346, .359, and—best of all—.394 in 1895, although that was only good enough for third place in the National League batting race. Playing in the dead-ball era, he also hit 17 home runs while driving in 80—both career highs—in 1893.

Clements, who was one of three people who briefly managed the Phillies in 1890 when regular skipper Harry Wright had physical problems, played one season each with the St. Louis Browns, Cleveland Spiders, and Boston Beaneaters at the end of his career, which concluded in 1900. He was the last lefthander to serve as a starting catcher.

Tom (Tido) Daly was another Philadelphia native who made a big splash in the big leagues. A catcher early in his career, he switched to second base after injuring his throwing arm. One of baseball's earliest switch-hitters, Daly is sometimes credited with the first pinch-hit home run in the major leagues, supposedly in 1892.

Daly put in 16 seasons in the majors, debuting in 1887 and departing in 1903. He began with the Chicago White Stockings, moved after two years to the Washington Nationals, where he and Connie Mack were the team's catchers, and one year later was traded to the Brooklyn Bridegrooms, a team for which he played in 11 seasons, including its three pennant winners. Daly jumped to the new American League's Chicago White Sox in 1902, then played briefly with the Cincinnati Reds at the end of his big league

Tom Daly

career the following year. He went on to play four more years in the minors.

Standing just 5 feet, 7 inches, Daly was a speedy runner who once swiped 51 bases in one season and another time pilfered 43. He led the National League in doubles in 1901 with 38. As Brooklyn's regular second baseman, Daly had five seasons over .300, including a .341 average in 1894. His lifetime batting average was .278.

Philadelphia also produced one of the best pre-20th-century pitchers in lefthander Matt Kilroy, a 10-year veteran with a 141–133 record that included one 46-win season. Kilroy broke in with the American Association's Baltimore Orioles in 1886, and in his rookie year struck out an all-time-record 513 batters and led the league with 68 appearances (all starts) and 66 complete games while posting a 29–34 record. That year, he hurled a one-hitter and a 16-

Matt Kilroy

strikeout two-hitter against the Athletics, winning the former, 1–0, and losing the latter, 3–0.

As if all that wasn't enough, Kilroy shattered the "sophomore jinx" by winning 46 games (19 losses) in the highest total ever recorded by a southpaw. He also led the league with 589 innings pitched while again leading the circuit in games (69), complete games (66), and shutouts (six). Twice during the season Kilroy won both ends of a doubleheader. His 75 triumphs in his first two seasons are the most wins in a pitcher's first two years in baseball history.

Plagued by arm trouble, Kilroy slipped to 17–21 in 1888. But he bounced back with a 29–25 mark the following year while leading his circuit with 55 complete games (of 56 starts). Kilroy jumped to the Players League in 1890, but more arm trouble waylaid his short stint with the Boston Reds. After the league dissolved, he pitched in five more seasons, but his arm was shot. While taking the mound for four different teams, Kilroy had just an 11–19 record before his big league career ended in 1898. Kilroy had hurled in 303 games, posting a 3.47 earned run average. In his final year he was a part-time leadoff hitter and outfielder for the Chicago Orphans of the National League.

Another player of considerable note was William (Kid) Gleason of Camden. Gleason gained prominence as a pitcher, as a second baseman, and finally as a manager. As a player, Gleason took the field during 20 big league seasons, plus small parts of two others. As a manager, he was the skipper of the ill-fated Chicago White Sox, otherwise known as the Black Sox.

Gleason began his career in 1888 as a pitcher with the Phillies. In his first four years he won 78 games (losing 70), including a club-record 38 (17 losses) in 1890. Before that season Gleason had jumped to the rebel Players League, but he was soon expelled when it was learned that he had also signed a contract for the season with the Phillies. Kid continued his fine pitching over the next four years, going 24–22, 20–24, and 21–22 with lowly St. Louis Browns teams and 17–11 with the Browns and Pittsburgh Pirates.

A serious arm injury in 1895, however, cost him dearly, and after compiling an overall 138–131 record with a 3.79 ERA, Gleason's career on the mound came to an end. Always a good hitter, he switched to second base, and for the next 12 years started for the Baltimore Orioles, New York Giants, Detroit Tigers, and then the Phillies, for whom he spent four years as the regular second sacker. Gleason hit .309 in 1895 and .319 in 1897, winding up his career with a .261 average with 1,944 hits. He was the last major leaguer to pitch 500 innings in one season and bat 500 times in another.

The first batting champion of a major league was a strong-hitting, weak-fielding third baseman/second baseman/outfielder

Kid Gleason

named Levi Meyerle, one of professional baseball's first Jewish players. Meyerle first saw the light of day in Philadelphia, and 26 years later, playing with one of the early incarnations of the Philadelphia Athletics in the brand new National Association's first season in 1871, he hit a staggering .492 (64-for-130) to lead the circuit in hitting. No league batting leader ever had a higher average. Meyerle also finished the first major league season with the lead in home runs (four) and slugging percentage (.700).

Clumsy as a fielder—he once made six errors in a single game—Meyerle never hit below .300 during seven seasons. His .365 career average included a .394 mark in 1874, when he again led the NA after jumping to the Chicago White Stockings. He also hit .349 and

Fred Dunlap

.340, and in 1876 was a participant in the first National League game while playing with another Athletics team at Philadelphia's Jefferson Park.

Another one of baseball's early .400 hitters also came from Philadelphia. In 1884, while playing for the first-place St. Louis Maroons in the Union Association, Fred Dunlap, who also managed the team, ran away with the batting title with a .412 average. The next closest player hit .364. Dunlap also led the league in hits (185), runs (160), home runs (13), and slugging percentage (.621) that year, and for the first of three times, topped all second basemen in fielding percentage.

Although he never came close to reaching his lofty average of 1884, many regarded Dunlap, or "Sure Shot" as he was nicknamed, as the finest player of his era and the best second baseman in the game. Appearing in 12 seasons, he had a lifetime average of .292. He was also an excellent base runner.

While playing from 1880 to 1891, Dunlap also wore the uniforms of the National League's Cleveland Blues, St. Louis Maroons (same name as the UA team), Detroit Wolverines, and Pittsburgh Alleghenys, and at the end of his career the New York Giants of the Players League and the Washington Nationals of the American Association. His most productive work came during the first four years of his career, which were spent with Cleveland. He hit .325 one year and .326 another.

Dunlap played a key role in an important rule change. In 1880 he hit an apparent home run with one man on base in the bottom of the ninth inning to break a scoreless tie. Under the existing "sudden death rule," Cleveland got a 1–0 victory, the game ending when the first runner reached the plate with Dunlap not getting credit for a home run. Two months later the National League changed the rule and awarded Dunlap his homer, giving the Blues a 2–0 triumph.

Wilmington contributed several outstanding pitchers in the 19th century, one being John (Sadie) McMahon, a pudgy righthander who toiled in nine seasons between 1889 and 1897 and compiled a 175–127 record with a 3.49 ERA. While hurling in the American Association, first with the Philadelphia Athletics and then with the Baltimore Orioles, Sadie led the league in wins twice, registering 36–21 and 34–25 logs.

A notorious hell-raiser, McMahon worked in more than 500 innings twice, leading the AA in that category as well as in complete games with 57 (out of 60 starts) and 58 (61 starts). Between 1892 and 1894 he won 69 more games with the National League's Orioles, going 20–25, 24–17, and 25–8. He wound up his career with the Brooklyn Bridegrooms, a shoulder injury writing a premature ending to his big league mound duty.

Another good hurler from Wilmington was Bert Cunningham, owner of a 142–167 record (4.22 ERA) while playing with six mostly bad big league teams during a 12-year career. Although hardly a control pitcher (he walked 1,064 batters in 2,727 innings), the junk-balling Cunningham had a 22–29 season in 1888 with the AA's Baltimore club and a 28–15 mark, including 11 straight wins, in 1898 with the Louisville Colonels of the NL. Incredibly, he spent four years in the minors in the midst of his career, at one point putting up a 35–20 record with Sioux City.

Duke Esper of Salem, New Jersey, was also a noteworthy pre-20th-century baseball player. Esper pitched from 1890 through 1898, recording a 101–100 mark with a 4.40 ERA in 237 games. He appeared in the uniforms of six teams, including the Phillies and the Philadelphia Athletics of the American Association. His best year was 1891 when he won 20 and lost 15 with the Phillies. Two years later he lost a league-leading 28 (12 wins) while hurling with the Washington Nationals. That year, Esper worked in 334⅓ innings. In 1895 he won the only game for the Baltimore Orioles in the Temple Cup series, beating the Cleveland Spiders, 5–0.

Gloucester, New Jersey, gave early baseball a standout third baseman in Bill Shindle. Usually right in the middle of the action, Shindle ranks among baseball's all-time third base leaders in putouts, chances, and assists. He once recorded 13 assists in a single game, which ties for the National League and major league record. Conversely, he also holds the major league record for most errors in one season set in 1890 when he committed 115 miscues while playing with the Philadelphia Quakers in the short-lived Players League. In 1892 he made five errors in one game.

Shindle played in 13 big league seasons, beginning in 1886 and ending in 1898. Along the way, while compiling a .269 career batting average, he played with the Detroit Wolverines, Baltimore Orioles, Phillies, and Brooklyn Bridegrooms of the National League, the American Association's Baltimore Orioles, and the Quakers.

Shindle, who had hit .314 in 1889, came up with his best year in 1890 when he punched out a .324 average with 10 home runs and 90 RBI for the Quakers in the PL's only year of existence. A regular during 11 seasons, Shindle's longest stint came with Brooklyn, where he played for five years after being part of an ill-advised trade that sent Wee Willie Keeler to Baltimore.

Al (Smiling Al) Maul pitched with success during his 15 seasons in the majors. The Philadelphia native won 84 and lost 80 with a 4.43 ERA in 187 games. Although he made his first big league appearance in 1884 with the Philadelphia Keystones of the Union Association, he did not pitch in the majors again until he joined the Phillies in 1887. Maul spent one year with the Phils, then moved on to play with five other teams before he was through in 1901.

Maul had big years in 1890, when he went 16–12 with the Pittsburgh Infants of the Players League, and in 1898, when he fashioned a 20–7 mark with the National League's Baltimore Orioles. In between, he won in double figures three other times. In 1893 he lost 21 games with the Washington Nationals. He led the NL with a 2.45 ERA in 1895.

Philadelphia also started Tom (Oyster) Burns on the way to big league stardom. A peppy outfielder who suited up in 11 big league seasons, he played primarily with the Baltimore Orioles of the American Association and the National League's Brooklyn Bridegrooms, who won three pennants during Burns's seven seasons with the club.

Burns was captain of the Orioles for a time, until he was relieved of his duties after throwing a ball at the opposing pitcher following a groundout. He had other blots on his reputation. Once, while trying to be funny, he tweaked teammate Tom Daly in the leg with his penknife while the catcher dozed in the outfield between games of a doubleheader. Awaking suddenly, Daly turned into the blade, severing a tendon.

Burns was a fine hitter who finished his career with a .300 average. He hit more than .300 four times—his high coming in 1887 when he compiled a .341 mark with Baltimore—and six other times went above .280. Burns led the American Association in triples (19) in 1887 and the National League in home runs (13) and RBI (128) in 1890.

In 1883, Burns's team, the Chicago White Stockings, scored a major-league-record 18 runs in one inning en route to a 26–6 rout of the Detroit Wolverines. Burns went 3-for-3 during the inning with two doubles and a home run. In another game a few years later Burns scored four runs without benefit of a hit.

Frank (Silver) Flint, noted as one of the best catchers of his day, never wore a glove—and as a result at one time or another broke every bone in his hands. He drew his first breath in Philadelphia before moving away as a youngster. Flint took the field for 12 years, playing in all but one of those seasons with the National League's

Chicago White Stockings. He managed the Sox for a short time in 1879 (5–12).

His career batting average was only .239, but, after hitting .167 the year before, Flint had a .310 season in 1881. He had had a .284 mark in 1879. Flint set a record for fewest career walks (53) of any nonpitcher who appeared in 10 or more seasons. He led all catchers in fielding percentage twice.

Another catcher from Philadelphia was Joe Sugden, who played in 12 seasons between 1893 and 1905. While posting a .255 career average, compiled mostly as a backup backstop, Sugden spent seven years in the National League, mostly with the Pittsburgh Pirates, and then jumped to the new American League where he spent most of his time with the St. Louis Browns. Sugden, then a coach, also suited up in 1912 as a replacement player for the "makeshift" Detroit Tigers in their game against the Philadelphia Athletics.

Many other 19th-century players came from the Philadelphia area. Here are some of the more prominent ones:

George (Orator) Shaffer came from Philadelphia and hit .283 during 11 big league seasons between 1874 and 1890. An outfielder, he played with 11 different teams in four different leagues. Most of his time was spent in the National League, with his longest stint being three years with the Cleveland Blues. He played with Philadelphia teams in both the National Association and the American Association. He reached highs at the plate of .360 and .338. In 1884, while playing with the St. Louis Maroons of the Union Association, he led the league in doubles with 40.

John (Jocko) Milligan was a catcher who sometimes played first base while putting in 10 years of service from 1884 to 1893. He hit .286 over that period, collecting averages of .303 one year and .302 another. He had a league-leading 35 doubles in 1891. Philadelphia born and bred, Milligan wore the uniform of the American Association's Philadelphia Athletics in his first four years in the big leagues and once again in 1891. The year before, he played with the Philadelphia Quakers of the Players League.

Mike Grady of Kennett Square made his debut as a backup catcher with the Phillies in 1894. He left the Phils in 1897, and before departing the big league scene in 1906 he had played with three other teams as a catcher and sometime first baseman. He reached a high of .334 in 86 games with the New York Giants in 1899, then hit .313 with the St. Louis Cardinals in 1904. In 11 seasons Grady had a career average of .294

William (Yank) Robinson, a Philadelphia-born outfielder/infielder, compiled a .241 lifetime average during 10 seasons, including five as the regular second baseman with the St. Louis Browns of the American Association. In 1889, Robinson's St. Louis teammates refused to play after Yank had been suspended for arguing vehemently with club owner Chris Von der Ahe. The dispute was settled without a strike. Robinson's career went from 1882 to 1892 and included stops with five other teams. He hit a career-high .305 in 1887, and he led the league in bases on balls three times. The weak-hitting Robinson set major league records in 1888 with 116 walks and the lowest batting average (.231) by a player who led the league in on-base percentage (.400). He led the league with 118 walks while collecting 94 hits and batting .208 the following year.

Albert (Doc) Bushong, a graduate of the University of Pennsylvania and a practicing dentist after his playing days ended, was a veteran of 12 big league campaigns, seven of which were spent in the National League with the Worcester Brown Stockings and the Cleveland Blues. Playing in the bigs between 1875 and 1890, the Philadelphia catcher was credited with pioneering the use of a padded glove. A light hitter with a .214 career average, Bushong's best years at the plate came between 1885 and 1887 when he went .267, .223, and .254 with the St. Louis Maroons. In 1886 he was the first backstop to go behind the plate 100 times in one season.

Dick Harley played with five different teams during seven big league seasons from 1897 to 1903. An outfielder from Philadelphia, he was a regular in six seasons. He had a career average of .262 with a high of .291—including one 6-for-6 game—in his rookie year with the National League's St. Louis Browns. In his next-to-last season he registered a .281 mark with the Detroit Tigers of the American League.

Jack Farrell out of Newark, Delaware, played in 11 seasons in the majors, most of the time as a reserve infielder. He hit .243 with 22 home runs while playing between 1879 and 1889 with five teams, including the 1886 Phillies. Farrell's best year was in 1883 when he hit .305 with the Providence Grays. In 1885 he was suspended without pay for yelling obscenities at fans.

Dick McBride of Philadelphia pitched in 237 games between 1871 and 1876 with the Philadelphia Athletics of the National Association and the Boston Red Caps of the National League. He compiled a 149–78 record with a 2.85 ERA. He had a 33–22 mark in 1884 when he led the National League in ERA, and a 44–14 log while working in 539 innings (1.97 ERA) in 1875. In 1871, during a 49–33 win by the Athletics over the Troy Haymakers, McBride scored seven runs.

Ed (Jersey) Blakey from Blackwood, New Jersey, went 77–125 with a 3.66 ERA in six seasons between 1883 and 1891. During that time he wore the uniform of nine different teams and in 1888 posted a 25–33 record with the AA's Cleveland Blues. In consecutive seasons, Blakey lost 30, 33, 22, and 25 games. He played with Cleveland teams in three different leagues, including the Blues, the Spiders of the National League, and the Infants of the Players League.

Wes Fisler performed in six big league seasons, starting in 1871 with the Philadelphia Athletics of the National Association. That year, the Camden native led all first basemen in fielding percentage with a .972 mark. A second baseman sometimes, Fisler hit .350 in 1872, .344 the following year, and .328 in 1874 while still with the Athletics. He ended his career in 1876 with another Athletics team in the first year of the National League, finishing with a .310 batting average in 273 games.

Among others who stood above the crowd were an assortment of Philadelphians. Pitcher Jim (Hardie) Henderson had seasons of 27–23 and 25–35 en route to a career record of 81–121 with a 3.50 ERA in 210 games while working between 1883 and 1888 for four teams, including the Phillies, Baltimore Orioles, Brooklyn Grays, and Pittsburgh Alleghenys. Later an umpire, he died at the age of 41 after being hit by a trolley in Philadelphia.

Henry Boyle was a National League hurler from 1884 to 1889, appearing in 207 games and compiling an 89–111 record, including four seasons with more than 20 losses, and a 3.06 ERA with three teams. He played with the St. Louis Maroons (both AA and NL) and the Indianapolis Hoosiers.

Bill (Cherokee) Fisher appeared in 165 games with six teams between 1871 and 1878, checking in with a 57–84 record and a 2.83 ERA, and twice leading the league in that category with 1.80 and 1.81 marks. He is credited with serving the first National League home run, an inside-the-park blast by the Chicago White Stockings' Ross Barnes in 1876 in Cincinnati.

Sam Weaver went 67–80 with a 3.22 ERA in 152 games spread over five seasons between 1875 and 1886. He hurled a no-hitter in 1878, giving the Milwaukee Grays their first National League victory. That same year, however, he lost 31 games (12 wins) as his teammates averaged six errors per game behind him.

And John (Phenomenal) Smith, who gave himself his nickname, took the mound in 149 games for eight teams, including the AA's Athletics and the Phillies, between 1884 and 1891, attaining a career record of 57–78 and a 3.87 ERA. In his first big league game

Smith lost an 18–5 decision—all the runs being unearned—when his Brooklyn Grays teammates, unhappy with the lefthander's constant bragging, committed 14 errors, allegedly on purpose. The guilty players were each fined $500, but Smith was released in an attempt by Brooklyn ownership to restore harmony to the team.

9

Strongly Represented

Why Have So Many Major Leaguers Come from the Philadelphia Area?

aseball in the Philadelphia area is not something that can be taken lightly. The sport is one of the region's most significant institutions, and it has been for more than 150 years.

Let's go back to the beginning. The first time baseball was known to have been played in Philadelphia was in 1833, a date that by one-half dozen years precedes the popular notion of when the game was invented. The sport was called base ball or town ball in those days, and by all accounts it varied substantially from today's finely tuned version.

The popularity of baseball increased rapidly during the ensuing years, and by the 1860s amateur teams, most of them emanating from clubs and some of them formed by African American players, were appearing throughout the area. In one of the first recorded games, a team known as Equity defeated Pennsylvania, 65–52. At about the same time, Union soldiers fighting in the Civil War played the game while encamped in Philadelphia.

In 1865, Philadelphia etched its name in baseball history when a team called the Athletics signed the sport's first professional player, a lefthanded second baseman born in England. His name was Al Reach, and his pay was $1,000 for the season. Reach would become a prominent local figure, first as the owner of a successful sporting goods company and later as the first owner of the Philadelphia Phillies.

The first professional baseball league—the National Association—was formed in 1871, and another Philadelphia team called the Athletics won the circuit's first championship. Four years later, while pitching for the Athletics, Joe Borden, a New Jersey native who lived in Yeadon, and later West Chester, hurled the first no-hitter in professional baseball. Then, in 1876, after the National Association had folded, the National League was launched with yet another team called the Philadelphia Athletics as one of the charter members. The first National League game was played in Philadelphia at Jefferson Park, located at 25th and Jefferson Streets. Borden, now playing with Boston, was the winning pitcher.

Another circuit considered a major league was formed in 1882. Called the American Association, one of its teams was a still different squad called the Athletics. Slugging Athletics first baseman Harry Stovey, a Philadelphian, won the league's first home run title. The following year, the remains of the National League's defunct Worcester Brown Stockings franchise were moved to Philadelphia and renamed the Phillies. The name would become the longest-running uninterrupted nickname in professional sports, and the team would still be playing in Philadelphia more than 120 years later.

Three major league teams—the Phillies, the AA's Athletics, and the Quakers of the Players League, a circuit formed by players who for one year staged a strike against the National League—played in the city in 1890. Eleven years later in 1901, with all except the National League having disappeared, another Philadelphia Athletics team was one of the original members of the newly formed American League. That team would go on to win nine pennants and five World Series before it was unceremoniously moved to Kansas City after the 1954 season.

That unfortunate shift notwithstanding, it is obvious that baseball has enjoyed a long and remarkable history in the Philadelphia area. Although baseball has wandered back and forth between highs and lows, it has for most of its years been the region's dominant sport as well as a central part of the area's social, economic, and recreational life.

The fact that the region has contributed some 350 players to the major leagues since 1900 supports that contention. The game has been so popular—and so conspicuous—during its lengthy existence that developing a relatively large number of big league players is a natural extension of its prominence.

Above and beyond that view, though, is the unavoidable question: Why? Why, in an area in the northeastern part of the country where snow, cold weather, and late-arriving springs hamper an outdoor sport such as baseball, has the Philadelphia region contributed what could be considered a substantial number of players to the big leagues?

Of course, the Philadelphia area's contribution does not compare favorably with those of the states in warm climates, such as California, Arizona, Texas, and Florida. In those areas, baseball is played throughout the year, and youngsters have an advantage when it comes to developing their skills.

Remarkably, however, when it comes to numbers of players born in Pennsylvania, the Keystone State has produced more major league baseball players during the sport's long history than every other state except California. According to Baseball-Reference. com, some 1,298 players were born in Pennsylvania while 1,697 came from California. Among other nearby states, New Jersey is the birthplace of 372 players, Delaware 47, Maryland 264, New York 1,073, and Ohio 928. Of the other warm-weather states, Texas follows California with 663, while Florida claims 286 and Arizona 62.

In addition to Pennsylvania's high statewide representation, in terms of producing major league players from large metropolitan areas, the Philadelphia area clearly has something special going for it. There are some obvious explanations.

"The fact that we had two major league clubs in Philadelphia for so many years helped to generate interest in the sport," said Skippy Wilson, who as head coach of the baseball team at Temple University for more than 40 years has sent in excess of 150 players into the pro ranks, including five to the major leagues. "For many years, the Phillies sponsored the 'Knot-Hole Gang,' and that plus special days at the ballpark for Cub Scouts, Little Leaguers, CYO, boys' clubs, and other such groups also contributed to the level of interest."

Baseball was especially popular in the Philadelphia area during the first half of the 20th century for another reason. Boys not only played in organized leagues, but also played on every possible open spot, whether it was a baseball field or a vacant lot. Moreover, when they weren't playing real baseball, they participated in other activities such as stickball, wallball, wireball, and various others—street games that were related to baseball.

"Baseball was especially big back in the 1920s, '30s, '40s, and '50s," reasoned Maje McDonnell, a member of the Phillies staff as a coach, batting practice pitcher, and front-office employee for more than 50 years. "During most of that time, there was no television, no radio; nearly everybody played baseball. And there were fields everywhere. In the summer, you played from the moment you got up until the moment you went to bed. Every neighborhood had a team as long as I can remember. And the older guys would take care of the younger guys, coaching them and helping them to learn the game. Most of the time, we played on playgrounds, and the playgrounds were jammed all day long."

"So many kids played baseball," said Wilson, born and raised in Philadelphia, "that through sheer numbers, there had to be many players come up through the ranks and make the pros."

"As a kid, you would dream about being a major leaguer," added Bobby Shantz, a fine big league pitcher for 16 seasons and the American League's Most Valuable Player in 1952. "I was small, and I didn't think I could make it. But my dad, like a lot of kids' parents, always wanted me and my brother [Wilmer] to be ballplayers, and he encouraged us a lot. We'd play all the time. Often we'd use cow dung for bases. And we had every kind of league. We even had a Sunday school league in Pottstown."

The Philadelphia area was such a baseball hotbed that for many years fast-paced semipro leagues with teams sponsored by various businesses were scattered throughout the area. Some players were so good that they turned down offers to play baseball in the minor or major leagues because they had soft jobs with the sponsoring companies, and with their work and baseball pay, they sometimes earned more than the average pro players.

In addition to the industrial leagues, other independent leagues such as the Penn-Del and the Delco Leagues flourished, as did American Legion ball. All drew a reasonably good number of spectators, and even attracted coverage in the local newspapers. Often, the rosters of teams in the adult leagues included players who had previously performed in organized baseball.

In the first half of the 20th century, baseball was the predominant professional sport in the Philadelphia area. Pro basketball was in its infancy, there was no major league ice hockey, and pro football was still a second-rate entity.

"Baseball was the main sport," said Marcus Hook native and two-time American League batting champion Mickey Vernon, who has a kids' league in Chester named after him. "So there was much more emphasis on the game, and that attracted a big number of kids."

And those who made it to the pros were idolized by kids from their neighborhoods. When a professional player, even if he performed in the low minors, would pass a group of boys assembled on the sidewalk, he was viewed with awe, and his name would be spoken in hushed tones like the kind reserved for deity. "Here comes Ralph," a kid would whisper as he and his friends worshipfully inspected every move, every stitch of clothing on the local hero. Even the neighborhood bullies would stop their antics to pay homage.

During the second half of the 20th century and into the 21st century, the common perception has been that baseball has had to share the spotlight with other sports and that its interest level has even been surpassed by many of them. Although football, basketball, soccer, ice hockey, and some other sports have cut into baseball's popularity, the perception is somewhat flawed. Baseball is not the feeble sport that many make it out to be.

While, sadly, the fields and playgrounds are often empty and many of the adult baseball leagues have been replaced by leagues playing the lesser game of softball, the sport continues to flourish in certain respects. And the Philadelphia area continues to send players to the major leagues in numbers that at least equal those of any other period. Witness the 22 local players who appeared with big league teams in 2001, 2002, and 2003.

"The game is as popular as any other in the area," insisted the New York Mets All-Star catcher Mike Piazza, who began playing baseball as a youth in Phoenixville. "It's something the area should be very proud of.

"The Philadelphia area has always been a great area for baseball," he claimed. "And in recent years, many high school and college teams have been very successful. Because of that success rate, the number of players attracted to pro careers has multiplied."

The one glaring exception is the astonishing lack in recent years of minority players from the area. Of the region's 22 recent big leaguers, just two represent a minority. The absence of African American players from the inner city is especially conspicuous considering the area's sizable black population.

While football and basketball have become the preferred sports of African Americans—substantially reducing their numbers in baseball—local baseball people provide additional explanations. "The opportunities are just not there in the inner city," said the Phillies' assistant general manager and director of scouting and development Mike Arbuckle, "so the kids quickly lose interest. They see African Americans playing basketball and football and appearing on television in big commercials, and we lose them even before they reach high school. And we're losing them in droves."

Even when they do reach high school, the chances of playing a decent brand of baseball are slim to none. With the exception of a few programs, high school baseball in the inner city, because of—for various reasons—an absence of resources, lacks adequate playing fields and equipment, and the level of coaching is exceptionally poor. And, although the Phillies operate a highly successful baseball program for inner-city youth, other summer programs with one other exception simply don't exist. So black (and white and Hispanic) baseball players, unless they're from the outer areas of the city or from the suburbs, have little chance to develop.

Meanwhile, the opportunities for players from the suburbs to develop are abundant. Not only are most of the high school programs more than adequate, but summer programs that kindle a kid's interest and nurture his talent are, too. Simply stated, it's all there if a boy wants it.

"Look at all the teams in the area," said the Philadelphia-born McDonnell. "There is Little League, Babe Ruth League, Connie Mack League, and a number of other leagues. We didn't have them when I was a boy. There are more high schools than ever, and they're all playing baseball. Some of them really focus on baseball. Plus, colleges are giving out huge numbers of scholarships and playing bigger schedules."

The schedules of local colleges haven't reached the levels of those in warmer climates, but that limitation may be something of an advantage, according to Bristol native Joe McEwing, an infielder with the Mets and previously the St. Louis Cardinals.

"Although we don't get to play as many high school or college games in the region as they do in the warmer climates," said McEwing, who began playing T-ball at the age of five, "players from the Northeast are not as worn out as kids who play 60 or 70 games a season in the South or Southwest. So local kids don't get burned out as early. They have lots of baseball left in them, and they probably peak later."

Conversely, Joe Kerrigian thinks that the shorter high school and college schedules are a handicap for local players, who have far fewer at-bats or games pitched. But, said the former big league pitcher and manager, there was a time when he was growing up that a local player, if he played in several different leagues, could get all the playing time he wanted, and that opportunity was a decided benefit to his professional aspirations.

"'In the 1960s, '70s, and before, you could always play 10 games a week in the Philadelphia area if you wanted to," said Kerrigan, the Phillies pitching coach and another Philadelphia native. "And there were a lot of great leagues in and around the city. There was some real good competition, and you played against some of the better players in the region. That played a big part in your development as a player."

Even in recent years, though, baseball has played an important role in the production and development of local players. No one knows that better than Ruben Amaro, the Phillies assistant general manager and former big league player who was raised in Philadelphia and—with his father having been a major league player—has had a connection with baseball since he was born.

"Obviously, baseball has been a huge part of my life," Amaro said. "It would be foreign to me to think about life without baseball. Beyond the personal aspect, I think that sports is a huge part of life in this area. People can talk about the popularity of baseball in Florida and Texas and California, and obviously many athletes come from those areas.

"But there's a rich tradition of baseball in the whole northeast part of the country. This is particularly true of the Philadelphia area. A lot of it has to do with children going out and playing baseball and watching it. If you didn't play baseball when I was growing up, you were kind of out of the loop. And it's not much different today."

There are, of course, many differences in baseball today, including the way it's played, its degree of popularity compared with other sports, the financial aspects of the game, and numerous other factors. But baseball, as it has always been, remains a strong staple of the local sports scene. And with that comes more players for the major leagues.

As an area that is far less likely to produce professional players than others, the Philadelphia region has had no shortage of homegrown major leaguers. They've reached that level for a variety of reasons. Collectively, they add to the list of significant contributions by the Philadelphia area.

10
The Best of the Best

Facts, Figures, and League Leaders (Since 1900)

HALL OF FAME MEMBERS

Herb Pennock, 1948
Joe McCarthy, 1957
Goose Goslin, 1968
Roy Campanella, 1969
Reggie Jackson, 1993
Tom Lasorda, 1997

MOST VALUABLE PLAYERS (LEAGUE)

Bucky Walters, Cincinnati Reds, 1939 (27–11, 2.29)
Roy Campanella, Brooklyn Dodgers 1951 (.325–33–108), 1953
 (.312–41–142), 1955 (.318–32–107)
Bobby Shantz, Philadelphia Athletics, 1952 (24–7, 2.48)
Reggie Jackson, Oakland Athletics, 1973 (.293–32–117)

20-Game Winners

Ray Caldwell, Cleveland Indians, 1919 (20–10)
Herb Pennock, New York Yankees, 1924 (21–9), 1926 (23–11)
Bucky Walters, Cincinnati Reds, 1939 (27–11), 1940 (22–10),
    1944 (23–8)
Bobby Shantz, Philadelphia Athletics, 1952 (24–7)
Mark Gubicza, Kansas City Royals, 1988 (20–8)
John Smiley, Pittsburgh Pirates, 1991 (20–8)
Jamie Moyer, Seattle Mariners, 2001 (20–6)

No-Hitters

Ray Caldwell, Cleveland Indians, September 10, 1919, vs. New
    York
Bill Dietrich, Chicago White Sox, June 1, 1937, vs. St. Louis
Bill McCahan, Philadelphia Athletics, September 3, 1947, vs.
    Washington

Rookies of the Year

Del Ennis, Philadelphia Phillies, 1946
Jon Matlack, New York Mets, 1972
Jeff Leonard, San Francisco Giants, 1979
Mike Piazza, Los Angeles Dodgers, 1993

Other Most Valuable Player Winners

Reggie Jackson, Oakland Athletics, 1973 World Series
Jon Matlack, New York Mets, 1975 All-Star Game (co-MVP)
Reggie Jackson, New York Yankees, 1977 World Series
Jeff Leonard, San Francisco Giants, 1987 League Championship
    Series
Mike Piazza, Los Angeles Dodgers, 1996 All-Star Game

Unassisted Triple Play

Ernie Padgett, Boston Braves, October 6, 1923, vs. Philadelphia

League Leaders

Hitting

HOME RUNS

Harry Davis, Philadelphia Athletics, 1904 (10), 1905 (8),
   1906 (12), 1907 (8)

Reggie Jackson, Oakland Athletics, 1973 (32), 1975 (36);
   New York Yankees, 1980 (41); California Angels, 1982 (39)

BATTING AVERAGE

Goose Goslin, Washington Senators, 1928 (.379)

Mickey Vernon, Washington Senators, 1946 (.353), 1953 (.337)

RBI

Harry Davis, Philadelphia Athletics, 1905 (83), 1906 (96)

Goose Goslin, Washington Senators, 1924 (129)

Del Ennis, Philadelphia Phillies, 1950 (126)

Roy Campanella, Brooklyn Dodgers, 1953 (142)

Reggie Jackson, Oakland Athletics, 1973 (117)

RUNS

Roy Thomas, Philadelphia Phillies, 1900 (132)

Harry Davis, Philadelphia Athletics, 1905 (93)

Reggie Jackson, Oakland Athletics, 1969 (123), 1973 (99)

DOUBLES

Harry Davis, Philadelphia Athletics, 1902 (43), 1905 (47),
   1907 (35)

Tom Daly, Brooklyn Bridegrooms, 1901 (38) (tie)

Mickey Vernon, Washington Senators, 1946 (51), 1953 (43),
   1954 (33)

TRIPLES

Bill Hinchman, Pittsburgh Pirates, 1916 (16)

Goose Goslin, Washington Senators, 1923 (18), 1925 (20)

SLUGGING PERCENTAGE

Reggie Jackson, Oakland Athletics, 1969 (.608), 1973 (.531);
Baltimore Orioles, 1976 (.502)

Pitching

WINS

Bucky Walters, Cincinnati Reds, 1939 (27), 1940 (22)

Bobby Shantz, Philadelphia Athletics, 1952 (24)

John Smiley, Pittsburgh Pirates, 1991 (20)

EARNED RUN AVERAGE

Bucky Walters, Cincinnati Reds, 1939 (2.29), 1940 (2.48)

Bobby Shantz, New York Yankees, 1957 (2.45)

WINNING PERCENTAGE

Herb Pennock, New York Yankees, 1923 (.760)

Bobby Shantz, Philadelphia Athletics, 1952 (.774)

John Smiley, Pittsburgh Pirates, 1991 (.714)

SAVES

Jack Meyer, Philadelphia Phillies, 1955 (16)

Ray Narleski, Cleveland Indians, 1955 (19)

Rawley Eastwick, Cincinnati Reds, 1975 (22), 1976 (26)

INNINGS PITCHED

Herb Pennock, New York Yankees, 1925 (277)

Bucky Walters, Cincinnati Reds, 1939 (319), 1940 (305),
1941 (302)

STRIKEOUTS

Bucky Walters, Cincinnati Reds, 1939 (137)

SHUTOUTS

Jon Matlack, New York Mets, 1976 (7)

GAMES STARTED

Bucky Walters, Cincinnati Reds, 1939 (31), 1940 (29), 1941 (27)

GAMES PITCHED

Ray Narleski, Cleveland Indians, 1955 (60)

Fielding

FIELDING AVERAGE

Roy Thomas, Philadelphia Phillies, OF, 1906 (.986)

Amos Strunk, OF, Philadelphia Athletics, 1912 (.990), 1914 (.987), 1917 (.986), 1918 (.988)

Buck Weaver, Chicago White Sox, 3B, 1917 (.949)

Jimmy Dykes, Philadelphia Athletics, 3B, 1932 (.980)

Mickey Vernon, Washington Senators–Cleveland Indians, 1B, 1950 (.991); Washington Senators, 1951 (.994), 1952 (.993), 1954 (.992)

Pat Kelly, Chicago White Sox, OF, 1975 (.991)

Dion James, Atlanta Braves, OF, 1987 (.996)

11

Everyone Who Played

A Complete List of 20th- and 21st-Century
Major League Players from the Philadelphia Region
(Through the 2002 Season)

PITCHERS

Name	Birthplace	Years Played	Teams	G	W	L	ERA	S*
Joe Bontikowski	Philadelphia	1962	Minnesota	30	5	7	3.88	—
Carroll Brown	Woodbury, NJ	1911–15	Philadelphia (AL), New York (AL)	133	40	39	3.47	1
Mike Brown	Camden	1982–87	Boston, Seattle	61	12	20	5.75	—
Bob Buchanan	Ridley Park	1985, 1989	Cincinnati, Kansas City	16	1	0	9.78	—
Elmer Burkart	Philadelphia	1936–39	Philadelphia (NL)	16	1	1	4.93	—
Ralph Caldwell	Philadelphia	1904–05	Philadelphia (NL)	13	3	5	4.20	1
Ray Caldwell	Croydon	1910–21	New York, Boston, Cleveland (all AL)	343	134	120	3.22	8

PITCHERS (Continued)

Name	Birthplace	Years Played	Teams	G	W	L	ERA	S*
Andy Carter	Philadelphia	1994–95	Philadelphia	24	0	2	4.75	—
Joe Cascarella	Philadelphia	1934–38	Philadelphia, Boston, Washington (all AL), Cincinnati	143	27	48	4.84	8
Pete Cimino	Philadelphia	1965–68	Minnesota, California	86	5	8	3.07	5
Mike Clark	Camden	1952–53	St. Louis (NL)	35	3	0	5.31	1
Lance Clemons	Philadelphia	1971–72, 1974	Kansas City, Boston, St. Louis	19	2	1	6.06	—
Jack Crimian	Philadelphia	1951–52, 1956–57	St. Louis (NL), Kansas City, Detroit	74	5	9	6.36	4
Bill Crouch, Jr.	Wilmington	1939, 1941, 1945	Brooklyn, Philadelphia, St. Louis (all NL)	50	8	5	3.47	7
Bert Cunningham	Wilmington	1887–91, 1895–1901	Brooklyn (AA), Baltimore (AA), Philadelphia (PL), Buffalo (PL), Louisville (NL), Chicago (NL)	341	142	167	4.22	2
Bill Dietrich	Philadelphia	1933–48	Philadelphia, Washington, Chicago (all AL)	366	108	128	4.48	11
Paul Doyle	Philadelphia	1969–70, 1972	Atlanta, San Diego, California	87	5	3	3.79	11
Rawley Eastwick	Camden	1974–81	Cincinnati, St. Louis, Philadelphia, Chicago (NL), New York (AL), Kansas City	326	28	27	3.31	68
Charlie Eckert	Philadelphia	1919–20, 1922	Philadelphia (AL)	25	0	3	4.52	—
Vaughn Eshelman	Philadelphia	1995–97	Boston	83	15	9	6.07	—
Bob File	Philadelphia	2001–02	Toronto	65	5	4	3.94	—

Name	Birthplace	Years Played	Teams	G	W	L	ERA	S*
Tom Filer	Philadelphia	1982, 1985, 1988–90, 1992	Chicago (NL), New York (NL), Toronto, Milwaukee	67	22	17	4.25	—
Pete Filson	Darby	1982–87, 1990	Minnesota, Chicago (AL), New York (AL), Kansas City	148	15	18	4.18	4
Scott Forster	Philadelphia	2000	Montreal	42	0	1	7.88	—
Casey Fossum	Cherry Hill, NJ	2001–02	Boston	56	8	6	3.87	1
Wayne Franklin	Wilmington	2000–02	Houston, Milwaukee	40	2	1	4.55	—
Steve Frey	Meadowbrook	1989–96	Montreal, San Francisco, Philadelphia, California, Seattle	314	18	15	3.76	28
Eddie Gaillard	Camden	1997–98	Detroit, Tampa Bay	22	1	0	5.46	1
Dan Gakeler	Mount Holly, NJ	1991	Detroit	31	1	4	5.74	2
Bob Gibson	Philadelphia	1983–87	Milwaukee, New York (NL)	98	12	18	4.24	13
Dallas Green	Newport, DE	1960–67	Philadelphia, Washington, New York (NL)	185	20	22	4.26	4
Nelson Greene	Philadelphia	1924–25	Brooklyn	15	2	1	8.71	1
Mark Gubicza	Philadelphia	1984–97	Kansas City, Anaheim	384	132	136	3.96	2
Buddy Harris	Philadelphia	1970–71	Houston	22	1	1	6.32	—
Fred Heimach	Camden	1920–26, 1928–33	Philadelphia, Boston, New York (all AL), Brooklyn	296	62	69	4.46	7
Frank Hoerst	Philadelphia	1940–42, 1946–47	Philadelphia (NL)	98	10	33	5.17	1
Joe Hudson	Philadelphia	1995–98	Boston, Milwaukee	102	6	7	4.82	2
Sig Jakucki	Camden	1936, 1944–45	St. Louis (AL)	72	25	22	3.79	5
Bill Johnson	Wilmington	1983–84	Chicago (NL)	14	1	0	3.57	—
Jing Johnson	Parker Ford	1916–17, 1919, 1927–28	Philadelphia (AL)	100	24	38	3.35	—

PITCHERS (Continued)

Name	Birthplace	Years Played	Teams	G	W	L	ERA	S*
Joel Johnston	West Chester	1991–95	Kansas City, Boston, Pittsburgh	59	3	5	4.31	2
Oscar Jones	London Grove	1903–05	Brooklyn	113	44	54	3.20	1
Ed Keegan	Camden	1959, 1961–62	Philadelphia, Kansas City	13	0	3	9.00	1
Hal Kelleher	Philadelphia	1935–38	Philadelphia (NL)	50	4	9	5.95	—
Joe Kerrigan	Philadelphia	1976–78, 1980	Montreal, Baltimore	131	8	12	3.89	15
Curtis King	Norristown	1997–99	St. Louis	68	6	2	3.43	2
Mike Koplove	Philadelphia	2001–02	Arizona	64	6	2	3.39	—
Lew Krausse, Jr.	Media	1961, 1964–74	Kansas City, Oakland, Milwaukee, Boston, St. Louis, Atlanta	321	68	91	4.00	21
Lew Krausse, Sr.	Media	1931–32	Philadelphia (AL)	23	5	1	4.50	—
Marty Kutyna	Philadelphia	1959–62	Kansas City, Washington	159	14	16	3.88	8
Tom Lasorda	Norristown	1954–56	Brooklyn, Kansas City	26	0	4	6.48	1
Bill Laxton	Camden	1970–71, 1974, 1976–77	Philadelphia, San Diego, Detroit, Seattle, Cleveland	121	3	10	4.73	5
Brett Laxton	Stratford, NJ	1999–2000	Oakland, Kansas City	9	0	2	7.86	—
Walt Masterson	Philadelphia	1939–42, 1945–53, 1956	Washington, Boston (AL), Detroit	399	78	100	4.15	20
Jon Matlack	West Chester	1971–83	New York (NL), Texas	361	125	126	3.18	3
Al Maul	Philadelphia	1884, 1887–91, 1893–1901	Philadelphia (UA & NL), Pittsburgh (PL & NL), Washington, Baltimore, Brooklyn, New York (all NL)	187	84	80	4.43	1
Bill McCahan	Philadelphia	1946–49	Philadelphia (AL)	57	16	14	3.84	—

Name	Birthplace	Years Played	Teams	G	W	L	ERA	S*
Jack McFetridge	Philadelphia	1890, 1903	Philadelphia (NL)	15	2	11	4.58	—
Brian Meyer	Camden	1988–90	Houston	34	0	5	2.84	2
Jack Meyer	Philadelphia	1955–61	Philadelphia	202	24	34	3.92	21
Gino Minutelli	Wilmington	1990–91, 1993	Cincinnati, San Francisco	27	0	3	5.31	—
Jamie Moyer	Sellersville	1986–2002	Chicago (NL), Texas, St. Louis, Baltimore, Boston, Seattle	439	164	125	4.14	—
Jeff Musselman	Doylestown	1986–90	Toronto, New York (NL)	142	23	15	4.31	3
Ray Narleski	Camden	1954–59	Cleveland, Detroit	266	43	33	3.60	58
Buster Narum	Philadelphia	1963–67	Baltimore, Washington	96	14	27	4.45	—
Blaine Neal	Marlton, NJ	2001–02	Florida	36	3	0	3.29	—
John O'Donoghue	Wilmington	1993	Baltimore	11	0	1	4.58	—
Curly Ogden	Ogden, PA	1922–26	Philadelphia (AL), Washington	93	18	19	3.79	—
Johnny Ogden	Ogden, PA	1918, 1928–29, 1931–32	New York (NL), Cincinnati, St. Louis (AL)	123	25	34	4.24	3
Herb Pennock	Kennett Square	1912–17, 1919–34	Philadelphia, Boston, New York (all AL)	617	241	162	3.60	33
Jim Peterson	Philadelphia	1931, 1933, 1937	Philadelphia (AL), Brooklyn	41	2	6	5.27	—
Johnny Podgajny	Chester	1940–43, 1946	Philadelphia (NL), Pittsburgh, Cleveland	115	20	37	4.20	—
George Prentiss	Wilmington	1901–02	Boston (AL), Baltimore	11	3	3	5.31	—
Ken Reynolds	Trevose	1970–73, 1975–76	Philadelphia, St. Louis, San Diego, Milwaukee	103	7	29	4.46	1
Lew Richie	Ambler	1906–13	Philadelphia, Boston, Chicago (all NL)	241	74	65	2.54	9
Dick Ricketts	Pottstown	1959	St. Louis	12	1	6	5.82	—

PITCHERS (Continued)

Name	Birthplace	Years Played	Teams	G	W	L	ERA	S*
George Riley	Philadelphia	1979–80, 1984, 1986	Chicago (NL), San Francisco, Montreal	41	1	5	4.97	—
Todd Rizzo	Media	1998–99	Chicago (AL)	12	0	2	12.38	0
Scott Schoeneweis	Long Branch, NJ	2000–02	Anaheim	144	27	30	5.27	1
Barney Schultz	Beverly, NJ	1955, 1959, 1961–65	St. Louis, Chicago (NL), Detroit	227	20	20	3.63	35
Socks Seibold	Philadelphia	1916–17, 1919, 1929–33	Philadelphia (AL), Boston (NL)	191	48	85	4.43	5
Frank Seward	Pennsauken, NJ	1943–44	New York (NL)	26	3	3	5.15	—
Bobby Shantz	Pottstown	1949–64	Philadelphia (AL & NL), Kansas City, New York (AL), Pittsburgh, Houston, St. Louis, Chicago (NL)	537	119	99	3.38	48
Roy Sherid	Norristown	1929–31	New York (AL)	87	23	24	4.71	7
Harry Shuman	Philadelphia	1942–44	Philadelphia (NL), Pittsburgh	30	0	0	4.44	—
John Smiley	Phoenixville	1986–97	Pittsburgh, Cincinnati, Minnesota, Cleveland	361	126	103	3.80	4
Edgar Smith	Columbus, NJ	1936–43, 1946–47	Philadelphia, Chicago, Boston (all AL)	282	73	113	3.82	12
Clyde Smoll	Quakertown	1940	Philadelphia (NL)	33	2	8	5.37	—
Ray Steineder	Salem, NJ	1923–24	Pittsburgh, Philadelphia (NL)	29	3	2	4.90	—
Dorn Taylor	Abington	1987, 1989–90	Pittsburgh, Baltimore	27	3	5	5.45	—
Tom Walker	Philadelphia	1902, 1904–05	Philadelphia (AL), Cincinnati	48	24	16	2.70	—
Augie Walsh	Wilmington	1927–28	Philadelphia (NL)	39	4	10	6.05	2

Name	Birthplace	Years Played	Teams	G	W	L	ERA	S*
Bucky Walters	Philadelphia	1934–48, 1950	Boston (NL), Philadelphia (NL), Cincinnati	428	198	160	3.30	4
Bryan Ward	Bristol	1998–2000	Chicago (AL), Philadelphia, Anaheim	95	1	3	5.09	1
Lefty Weinert	Philadelphia	1919–24, 1927–28, 1931	Philadelphia (NL), Chicago (NL), New York (AL)	131	18	33	4.59	2
Chris Welsh	Wilmington	1981–83, 1985–86	San Diego, Montreal, Texas, Cincinnati	122	22	31	4.45	—
Woody Wheaton	Philadelphia	1944	Philadelphia (AL)	11	0	1	3.55	—
Highball Wilson	Philadelphia	1899, 1902–04	Cleveland, Philadelphia (AL), Washington	47	14	26	3.29	—
Joe Yeager	Philadelphia	1898–1903	Brooklyn, Detroit	94	33	49	3.74	2
Stan Yerkes	Cheltenham	1901–03	Baltimore, St. Louis (NL)	45	15	24	3.66	—

*Although saves did not become an official category until 1961, statisticians have gone back and calculated saves for earlier pitchers.

CATCHERS

Name	Birthplace	Years Played	Teams	G	BA	HR	RBI	R	H
Harry Barton	Chester	1905	Philadelphia (AL)	29	.167	0	3	5	10
John Berger	Philadelphia	1922, 1927	Philadelphia (AL), Washington	11	.313	0	1	1	5
Sam Calderone	Beverly, NJ	1950, 1953–54	New York (NL), Milwaukee	91	.291	1	25	16	41
Doug Camilli	Philadelphia	1960–67, 1969	Los Angeles, Washington	313	.199	18	80	56	153
Roy Campanella	Philadelphia	1948–57	Brooklyn	1,215	.276	242	856	627	1,161
Jack Clements	Philadelphia	1884–1900	Philadelphia (NL & UA), St. Louis, Cleveland, Boston (all NL)	1,157	.286	77	687	619	1,226

CATCHERS (Continued)

Name	Birthplace	Years Played	Teams	G	BA	HR	RBI	R	H
Frank Crossin	Avondale	1912–14	St. Louis (AL)	55	.147	0	7	8	17
Benny Culp	Philadelphia	1942–44	Philadelphia (NL)	15	.192	0	2	5	5
Ben Davis	Chester	1998–2002	San Diego, Seattle	338	.242	26	144	121	260
Mike DiFelice	Philadelphia	1996–2002	St. Louis, Tampa Bay	422	.239	25	130	198	297
Jack Fimple	Darby	1983–84, 1986–87	Los Angeles, California	92	.228	2	28	21	45
Mike Grady	Kennett Square	1894–1901, 1904–06	Philadelphia, New York, St. Louis (all NL), Washington	918	.294	35	449	486	881
Bill Haeffner	Philadelphia	1915, 1920, 1928	Philadelphia (AL), Pittsburgh, New York (NL)	59	.194	0	14	8	35
Ron Henry	Chester	1961, 1964	Minnesota	42	.130	2	8	5	9
Jack Lapp	Frazer	1908–16	Philadelphia (AL), Chicago (AL)	567	.263	5	166	168	416
Jesse Levis	Philadelphia	1992–99, 2001	Cleveland, Milwaukee (AL & NL)	319	.255	3	60	66	167
John Marzano	Philadelphia	1987–92, 1995–98	Boston, Texas, Seattle	301	.241	11	72	79	191
Harry O'Donnell	Philadelphia	1927	Philadelphia (NL)	16	.063	0	2	1	1
Bob Peterson	Philadelphia	1906–07	Boston (AL)	43	.191	1	9	11	25
Mike Piazza	Norristown	1992–2002	Los Angeles, Florida, New York (NL)	1,393	.321	347	1,073	851	1,641
Dave Ricketts	Pottstown	1963, 1965, 1967–70	St. Louis, Pittsburgh	130	.249	1	20	15	53
Mike Scioscia	Upper Darby	1980–92	Los Angeles	1,441	.259	68	446	398	1,131
Wilmer Shantz	Pottstown	1954–55, 1960	Philadelphia (AL), Kansas City, New York (AL)	131	.257	2	29	31	98

Name	Birthplace	Years Played	Teams	G	BA	HR	RBI	R	H
Al Spohrer	Philadelphia	1928–35	New York (NL), Boston (NL)	756	.259	6	199	213	575
Joe Sugden	Philadelphia	1893–99, 1901–05, 1912	Pittsburgh, St. Louis (NL), Cleveland (NL), Chicago (AL), St. Louis (AL), Detroit	835	.255	3	283	303	696
Hal Wagner	Riverton, NJ	1937–44, 1946–49	Philadelphia (AL), Boston (AL), Detroit, Philadelphia (NL)	672	.248	15	228	179	458
Bill Warwick	Philadelphia	1921, 1925–26	Pittsburgh, St. Louis (NL)	23	.304	1	8	8	17
Chris Widger	Wilmington	1995–2000, 2002	Seattle, Boston, Montreal, New York (AL)	488	.242	50	188	147	361
Jimmie Wilson	Philadelphia	1923–40	Philadelphia (NL), St. Louis (NL), Cincinnati	1525	.284	32	621	580	1,358
Robbie Wine	Norristown	1986–87	Houston	23	.146	0	0	3	6

INFIELDERS

Name	Birthplace	Years Played	Teams	G	BA	HR	RBI	R	H
Wayne Ambler	Abington	1937–39	Philadelphia (AL)	271	.224	0	73	60	175
Joe Berry, Jr.	Philadelphia	1921–22	New York (NL)	15	.333	0	2	0	2
Frank Betcher	Philadelphia	1910	St. Louis (NL)	35	.202	0	6	7	18
Lena Blackburne	Clifton Heights	1910, 1912, 1914–15, 1918–19, 1927, 1929	Chicago (AL), Cincinnati, Boston, Philadelphia (all NL)	550	.214	4	139	173	387

INFIELDERS (Continued)

Name	Birthplace	Years Played	Teams	G	BA	HR	RBI	R	H
Al Brancato	Philadelphia	1939–41, 1945	Philadelphia (AL)	282	.214	4	80	117	199
Joe Burns	Bryn Mawr	1943–45	Boston (NL), Philadelphia (AL)	111	.230	2	16	24	69
Charlie Carr	Coatesville	1898, 1901, 1903–06, 1914	Washington (NL), Cincinnati, Philadelphia (AL), Detroit, Cleveland, Indianapolis (FL)	507	.252	6	240	185	492
Sean Casey	Willingboro	1997–2002	Cleveland, Cincinnati	651	.302	17	368	342	708
Joe Cassidy	Chester	1904–05	Washington	303	.228	2	76	130	264
Pete Childs	Philadelphia	1901–02	St. Louis, Chicago, Philadelphia (all NL)	212	.212	0	47	60	147
Ed Cihocki	Wilmington	1932–33	Philadelphia (AL)	34	.143	0	9	6	14
Bert Conn	Philadelphia	1898, 1900–01	Philadelphia (NL)	12	.267	0	2	7	8
Wid Conroy	Camden	1901–11	Milwaukee (AL), Pittsburgh, New York (AL), Washington	1,374	.248	22	452	605	1,257
Monte Cross	Philadelphia	1892, 1894–1907	Baltimore, Pittsburgh, St. Louis, Philadelphia (all NL), Philadelphia (AL)	1,682	.234	31	621	718	1,364
Tom Daly	Philadelphia	1887–96, 1898–1903	Chicago, Washington, Brooklyn (all NL), Chicago (AL), Cincinnati	1,564	.278	49	811	1,024	1,582

Name	Birthplace	Years Played	Teams	G	BA	HR	RBI	R	H
Harry Davis	Philadelphia	1895–99, 1901–17	New York, Pittsburgh, Louisville, Washington (all NL), Philadelphia (AL), Cleveland	1,755	.277	75	951	1,001	1,841
Jimmy Dykes	Philadelphia	1918–39	Philadelphia, Chicago (both AL)	2,282	.280	108	1,071	1,108	2,256
Lee Elia	Philadelphia	1966, 1968	Chicago (AL), Chicago (NL)	95	.203	3	25	17	43
Roy Ellam	West Conshohocken	1909, 1918	Cincinnati, Pittsburgh	36	.143	1	6	13	14
Eddie Feinberg	Philadelphia	1938–39	Philadelphia (NL)	16	.184	0	0	2	7
Harry Fritz	Philadelphia	1913–15	Philadelphia (AL), Chicago (FL)	149	.227	3	39	44	96
Shawn Gilbert	Camden	1997–98, 2000	New York (NL), St. Louis, Los Angeles	51	.149	2	4	9	7
Harry Gleason	Camden	1901–05	Boston (AL), St. Louis (AL)	274	.218	3	90	88	206
Kid Gleason	Camden	1888–1908, 1912 (also pitched before 1900)	Philadelphia, New York, Baltimore, St. Louis (all NL), Detroit, Chicago (AL)	1,966	.261	15	823	1,020	1,944
Billy Harrell	Norristown	1955, 1957–58, 1961	Cleveland, Boston (AL)	173	.231	8	26	54	79
Don Hasenmayer	Roslyn	1945–46	Philadelphia (NL)	11	.100	0	1	1	3
Lefty Herring	Philadelphia	1899, 1904	Washington (NL & AL)	17	.191	0	2	4	9
Harry Hinchman	Philadelphia	1907	Cleveland	15	.216	0	9	3	11
Brook Jacoby	Philadelphia	1981, 1983–92	Atlanta, Cleveland, Oakland	1,311	.270	120	545	535	1,220

INFIELDERS (Continued)

Name	Birthplace	Years Played	Teams	G	BA	HR	RBI	R	H
Chick Keating	Philadelphia	1913–15, 1926	Chicago, Philadelphia (both NL)	30	.089	0	0	4	4
Pat F. Kelly	Philadelphia	1991–99	New York (AL), St. Louis, Toronto	681	.249	36	217	253	495
John Knight	Philadelphia	1905–07, 1909–13	Philadelphia, Boston, New York, Washington (all AL)	767	.239	14	270	301	636
Chuck Kress	Philadelphia	1947, 1949–50, 1954	Cincinnati, Chicago (AL), Detroit, Brooklyn	175	.249	1	52	57	116
Ed Lennox	Camden	1906, 1909–10, 1912, 1914–15	Philadelphia (AL), Brooklyn, Chicago (NL), Pittsburgh (FL)	448	.274	18	185	138	379
Hans Lobert	Wilmington	1903, 1905–17	Pittsburgh, Chicago, Cincinnati, Philadelphia, New York (all NL)	1,317	.274	32	482	640	1,252
Carlton Lord	Philadelphia	1923	Philadelphia (NL)	17	.234	0	2	3	11
John Mabry	Wilmington	1994–2002	St. Louis, Seattle, San Diego, Florida, Philadelphia, Oakland	1,924	.271	66	328	292	699
Jeff Manto	Bristol	1990–91, 1993, 1995–98, 2000	Cleveland, Philadelphia, Baltimore, Boston, Seattle, Detroit, New York (AL), Colorado	289	.230	31	97	97	164
Harry Marnie	Philadelphia	1940–42	Philadelphia (NL)	96	.221	0	15	19	49
Ramon Martinez	Philadelphia	1998–2002	San Francisco	368	.269	20	106	129	249
Emmett McCann	Philadelphia	1920–21, 1926	Philadelphia, Boston (both AL)	71	.227	0	18	19	44

Name	Birthplace	Years Played	Teams	G	BA	HR	RBI	R	H
Joe McEwing	Bristol	1998–2002	St. Louis, New York (NL)	470	.256	22	120	153	298
Eddie Miksis	Burlington, NJ	1944, 1946–58	Brooklyn, Chicago (NL), St. Louis (NL), Cincinnati, Baltimore	1,042	.236	44	228	383	722
Mike Moriarity	Camden	2002	Baltimore	8	.188	0	3	0	3
Danny Murphy	Philadelphia	1900–15	Philadelphia (AL), New York (NL), Brooklyn (FL)	1,496	.289	44	702	705	1,563
Danny Murtaugh	Chester	1941–1943, 1946–51	Philadelphia, Boston, Pittsburgh (all NL)	767	.254	8	219	263	661
Kevin Orie	West Chester	1997–99, 2002	Cincinnati, Florida, Chicago (NL)	316	.249	22	116	117	253
Patsy O'Rourke	Philadelphia	1908	St. Louis (NL)	53	.195	0	16	8	32
Ernie Padgett	Philadelphia	1923–27	Boston (NL), Cleveland	271	.266	1	81	84	223
Harry Pearce	Philadelphia	1917–19	Philadelphia (NL)	135	.208	0	29	42	88
Joe Redfield	Doylestown	1988, 1991	California, Pittsburgh	12	.100	0	0	1	2
Bob Rice	Philadelphia	1926	Philadelphia (NL)	19	.148	0	10	3	8
Craig Robinson	Abington	1972–77	Philadelphia, Atlanta, San Francisco	292	.219	0	42	80	157
Ed Roetz	Philadelphia	1929	St. Louis (AL)	16	.244	0	5	7	11
Gene Schall	Abington	1995–96	Philadelphia	52	.252	2	15	9	33
Rick Schu	Philadelphia	1984–91, 1996	Philadelphia, Montreal, Baltimore, Detroit, California	580	.246	41	134	189	386
Bud Sharpe	West Chester	1905, 1910	Boston (NL), Pittsburgh	165	.222	0	41	40	139
Wally Smith	Philadelphia	1911–12, 1914	St. Louis (NL), Washington	201	.229	2	53	56	117

INFIELDERS (Continued)

Name	Birthplace	Years Played	Teams	G	BA	HR	RBI	R	H
Eddie Stanky	Philadelphia	1943–53	Chicago, Brooklyn, Boston, New York, St. Louis (all NL)	1,259	.268	29	364	811	1,154
Alan Strange	Philadelphia	1934–35, 1940–42	St. Louis (AL), Washington	314	.223	1	89	93	211
Ken Szotkiewicz	Wilmington	1970	Detroit	47	.107	3	9	9	9
Mickey Vernon	Marcus Hook	1939–43, 1946–60	Washington, Cleveland, Boston (AL), Milwaukee, Pittsburgh	2,409	.286	172	1,311	1,196	2,495
Bucky Walters	Philadelphia	1931–48, 1950	Boston (NL & AL), Philadelphia (NL), Cincinnati	715	.243	23	234	227	477
Joe Ward	Philadelphia	1906, 1909–10	Philadelphia (NL), New York (AL)	166	.237	0	47	47	110
Buck Weaver	Pottstown	1912–20	Chicago (AL)	1,254	.272	21	420	623	1,308
Ed Whited	Bristol	1989	Atlanta	36	.162	1	4	5	12
Joe Yeager	Philadelphia	1898–1903, 1905–08	Brooklyn, Detroit, New York (AL), St. Louis (AL)	574	.252	4	201	204	467
Steve Yerkes	Hatboro	1909, 1911–16	Boston (AL), Pittsburgh (FL), Chicago (NL)	711	.268	6	254	307	676
Ralph Young	Philadelphia	1913, 1915–22	New York, Detroit, Philadelphia (all AL)	1,022	.247	4	254	480	898

OUTFIELDERS

Name	Birthplace	Years Played	Teams	G	BA	HR	RBI	R	H
Cal Abrams	Philadelphia	1949–56	Brooklyn, Cincinnati, Pittsburgh, Baltimore, Chicago (AL)	567	.269	32	138	257	433
Ruben Amaro, Jr.	Philadelphia	1991–98	California, Philadelphia, Cleveland	485	.235	16	100	99	218
Cliff Brumbaugh	Wilmington	2001	Texas, Colorado	21	.217	1	4	6	10
Ted Cather	Chester	1912–15	St. Louis, Boston (both NL)	201	.252	2	72	60	138
Eddie Collins, Jr.	Lansdowne	1939, 1941–42	Philadelphia (AL)	132	.241	0	16	41	66
Jack Daniels	Chester	1952	Boston (NL)	106	.187	2	14	31	41
Brandy Davis	Newark, DE	1952–53	Pittsburgh	67	.187	0	3	19	25
Roy Elsh	Penns Grove, NJ	1923–25	Chicago (AL)	173	.262	0	39	55	106
Del Ennis	Philadelphia	1946–59	Philadelphia, St. Louis, Cincinnati (all NL), Chicago (AL)	1,903	.284	288	1,284	985	2,063
Tom Fleming	Philadelphia	1899, 1902, 1904	New York, Philadelphia (both NL)	30	.222	0	6	11	22
Walter French	Moorestown	1923, 1925–29	Philadelphia (AL)	397	.303	2	109	142	297
Purn Goldy	Camden	1962–63	Detroit	29	.231	3	12	9	18
Goose Goslin	Salem, NJ	1921–38	Washington, St. Louis (AL), Detroit	2,287	.316	248	1,609	1,483	2,735
Danny Green	Burlington	1898–1905	Chicago (NL), Chicago (AL)	923	.293	29	423	552	1,021
Bill Hallman	Philadelphia	1901, 1903, 1906–07	Milwaukee, Chicago (AL), Pittsburgh	319	.235	3	86	150	269

OUTFIELDERS (Continued)

Name	Birthplace	Years Played	Teams	G	BA	HR	RBI	R	H
Dick Harley	Philadelphia	1897–1903	St. Louis, Cleveland, Cincinnati (all NL), Detroit, Chicago (NL)	740	.262	10	236	389	755
Jack Hayden	Bryn Mawr	1901, 1906, 1908	Philadelphia, Boston (both AL), Chicago (NL)	147	.251	1	33	60	145
Bobby Higginson	Philadelphia	1995–2002	Detroit	1,091	.281	161	592	611	1,114
Hugh High	Pottstown	1913–18	Detroit, New York (AL)	516	.250	3	123	176	386
Bill Hinchman	Philadelphia	1905–09, 1915–18, 1920	Cincinnati, Cleveland, Pittsburgh	908	.261	20	369	364	793
Izzie Hoffman	Bridgeport	1904, 1907	Washington, Boston (NL)	29	.233	0	4	18	27
Keith Hughes	Bryn Mawr	1987–88, 1990, 1993	New York (AL), Baltimore, New York (NL), Cincinnati, Philadelphia	93	.204	2	24	18	41
Jim Jackson	Philadelphia	1901–02, 1905–06	Baltimore, Cleveland, New York (NL)	348	.235	4	132	159	300
Reggie Jackson	Wyncote	1967–87	Kansas City, Oakland, Baltimore, New York (AL), California	2,820	.262	563	1,702	1,551	2,584
Dion James	Philadelphia	1983–85, 1987–90, 1992–93, 1995–96	Milwaukee, Cleveland, New York (AL), Atlanta	917	.288	32	266	362	781
Jeff Jones	Philadelphia	1983	Cincinnati	16	.227	0	5	6	10

Name	Birthplace	Years Played	Teams	G	BA	HR	RBI	R	H
John Kelly	Clifton Heights	1907	St. Louis (NL)	53	.188	0	6	12	37
Pat Kelly	Philadelphia	1967–81	Minnesota, Kansas City, Chicago (AL), Baltimore, Cleveland	1,385	.264	76	418	620	1,147
Jeff Leonard	Philadelphia	1977–90	Los Angeles, Houston, San Francisco, Milwaukee, Seattle	1,415	.266	144	723	614	1,342
Howard Lohr	Philadelphia	1914, 1916	Cincinnati, Cleveland	21	.204	0	8	6	11
Bris Lord	Upland	1905–07, 1909–13	Philadelphia (AL), Cleveland, Boston (NL)	742	.256	13	236	379	707
Ralph Mattis	Philadelphia	1914	Pittsburgh (FL)	36	.247	0	8	14	21
Dave May	New Castle, DE	1967–78	Baltimore, Milwaukee, Atlanta, Texas, Pittsburgh	1,252	.251	96	422	462	920
Moose McCormick	Philadelphia	1904, 1908–09, 1912–13	New York, Pittsburgh, Philadelphia (all NL)	418	.285	6	133	165	356
Kevin Mench	Wilmington	2002	Texas	110	.260	15	60	52	95
Warren Miller	Philadelphia	1909, 1911	Washington	47	.188	0	1	8	16
Bobby Mitchell	Norristown	1970–71, 1973–75	New York, Milwaukee (both AL)	273	.235	21	91	86	143
Archie Moore	Upper Darby	1964–65	New York (AL)	40	.275	1	5	5	11
Jake Munch	Morton	1918	Philadelphia (AL)	22	.267	0	0	3	8
Scott Northey	Philadelphia	1969	Kansas City	20	.262	1	7	11	16
Alex Pitko	Burlington	1938–39	Philadelphia (NL), Washington	11	.259	0	3	2	7
Carl Powis	Philadelphia	1957	Baltimore	15	.195	0	2	4	8

OUTFIELDERS (Continued)

Name	Birthplace	Years Played	Teams	G	BA	HR	RBI	R	H
Eddie Silber	Philadelphia	1937, 1939	St. Louis (AL)	23	.310	0	4	10	26
Dick Spalding	Philadelphia	1927–28	Philadelphia (NL), Washington	131	.299	0	25	69	139
Al Spangler	Philadelphia	1959–71	Milwaukee, Houston, Chicago (all NL), California	912	.262	21	175	307	594
Amos Strunk	Philadelphia	1908–24	Philadelphia, Boston, Chicago (all AL)	1,512	.284	15	530	696	1,418
Pedro Swann	Wilmington	2000, 2002	Atlanta, Toronto	17	.071	0	1	3	1
Roy Thomas	Norristown	1899–1911	Philadelphia, Pittsburgh, Boston (all NL)	1470	.290	7	299	1,011	1,537
Kevin Ward	Lansdale	1991–92	San Diego	125	.217	5	20	25	55
Woody Wheaton	Philadelphia	1943–44	Philadelphia (AL)	37	.191	0	7	3	17

PLAYERS WHO APPEARED IN 10 GAMES OR FEWER

PITCHERS

Name	Birthplace	Years Played	Teams	G	W	L
John Barthold	Philadelphia	1904	Philadelphia (AL)	4	0	0
King Brady	Elmer, NJ	1905–08, 1912	Philadelphia, Pittsburgh, Boston (all NL), Boston (AL)	8	3	2
George Craig	Philadelphia	1907	Philadelphia (AL)	2	0	0
Bill Crouch, Sr.	Marshallton, DE	1910	St. Louis (AL)	1	0	0
Frank DiMichele	Philadelphia	1988	California	4	0	0
John Edelman	Philadelphia	1955	Milwaukee	5	0	0
Jake Eisenhart	Perkasie	1944	Cincinnati	1	0	0
Hilly Flitcraft	Woodstown, NJ	1942	Philadelphia (NL)	3	0	0

Name	Birthplace	Years Played	Teams	G	W	L
Keith Garagozzo	Camden	1994	Minnesota	7	0	0
Ed Gerner	Philadelphia	1919	Cincinnati	5	1	0
Paul Gilliford	Bryn Mawr	1967	Baltimore	2	0	0
Bill Grevell	Williamstown, NJ	1919	Philadelphia (AL)	5	0	0
Ray Hartranft	Quakertown	1913	Philadelphia (NL)	1	0	0
George Hesselbacher	Philadelphia	1916	Philadelphia (AL)	6	0	4
John Hobbs	Philadelphia	1981	Minnesota	4	0	0
Bill Hoffman	Philadelphia	1939	Philadelphia (NL)	3	0	0
Chick Holmes	Beverly, NJ	1918	Philadelphia (AL)	2	0	0
Bill Hughes	Philadelphia	1921	Pittsburgh	1	0	0
John Jackson	Wynnefield	1933	Philadelphia (NL)	10	2	2
Willie Jensen	Philadelphia	1912, 1914	Detroit, Philadelphia (AL)	6	1	3
Bill Kirk	Coatesville	1961	Kansas City	1	0	0
Bill Knowlton	Philadelphia	1920	Philadelphia (AL)	1	0	1
Dick Koecher	Philadelphia	1946–48	Philadelphia (NL)	7	0	4
Joe Kohlman	Philadelphia	1937–38	Washington	9	1	0
Bert Kuczynski	Philadelphia	1943	Philadelphia (AL)	6	0	1
Ed Lennon	Philadelphia	1928	Philadelphia (NL)	5	0	0
Pete Loos	Philadelphia	1901	Philadelphia (AL)	1	0	1
Sam Lowry	Philadelphia	1942–43	Philadelphia (AL)	6	0	0
Cy Malis	Philadelphia	1934	Philadelphia (NL)	1	0	0
John McGillen	Eddystone	1944	Philadelphia (AL)	2	0	0
Red Miller	Philadelphia	1923	Philadelphia (NL)	1	0	0
Joe Myers	Wilmington	1905	Philadelphia (AL)	1	0	0
Al Neiger	Wilmington	1960	Philadelphia (NL)	6	0	0
Joe Ohl	Jobstown, NJ	1909	Washington	4	0	0
Gil Paterson	Philadelphia	1977	New York (AL)	10	1	2
Pete Rambo	Thorofare, NJ	1926	Philadelphia (NL)	1	0	0
Chuck Ricci	Abington	1995	Philadelphia (NL)	7	1	0
Jack Ridgeway	Philadelphia	1914	Baltimore (FL)	4	0	1
Cliff Ross	Philadelphia	1954	Cincinnati	4	0	0
Al Smith	Norristown	1926	New York (NL)	1	0	0
Ad Swigler	Philadelphia	1917	New York (NL)	1	0	1
John Trautwein	Lafayette Hill	1988	Boston	9	0	1
Aloysius Travers	Philadelphia	1912	Detroit	1	0	1
Tink Turner	Swarthmore	1915	Philadelphia (AL)	1	0	1
Twink Twining	Horsham	1916	Cincinnati	1	0	0
Marty Walker	Philadelphia	1928	Philadelphia (NL)	1	0	1

PITCHERS (Continued)

Name	Birthplace	Years Played	Teams	G	W	L
Jesse Whiting	Philadelphia	1902, 1906–07	Philadelphia (NL), Brooklyn	5	1	2
Charley Young	Philadelphia	1915	Baltimore (FL)	9	2	3

CATCHERS

Name	Birthplace	Years Played	Teams	G	BA
Jeff Datz	Camden	1989	Detroit	7	.200
John Kalahan	Philadelphia	1903	Philadelphia (AL)	1	.000
Al Kenders	Barrington, NJ	1961	Philadelphia (NL)	10	.174
Joe Kracher	Philadelphia	1939	Philadelphia (NL)	5	.200
Mike Loan	Philadelphia	1912	Philadelphia (NL)	1	.500
Harry O'Neill	Philadelphia	1939	Philadelphia (AL)	1	—
Tony Parisse	Philadelphia	1943–44	Philadelphia (AL)	10	.143
Tom Patton	Honey Brook	1957	Baltimore	1	.000
Bill Peterman	Philadelphia	1942	Philadelphia (NL)	1	1.000
Butch Rementer	Philadelphia	1904	Philadelphia (NL)	1	.000
Jim Spotts	Honey Book	1930	Philadelphia (NL)	3	.000

INFIELDERS

Name	Birthplace	Years Played	Teams	G	BA
Ted Baldwin	Chadds Ford	1927	Philadelphia (NL)	6	.313
George Batten	Haddonfield, NJ	1912	New York (AL)	1	.000
Bill Black	Philadelphia	1924	Chicago (AL)	6	.200
Tom Chism	Chester	1979	Baltimore	6	.000
Press Cruthers	Marshallton, DE	1913–14	Philadelphia (AL)	7	.222
Jim Curry	Camden	1909, 1911, 1918	Philadelphia, New York, Detroit (all AL)	10	.229
Larry File	Chester	1940	Philadelphia (NL)	7	.077
Ed Irvin	Philadelphia	1912	Detroit	1	.667
John Karst	Philadelphia	1915	Brooklyn	1	—
Charlie Marshall	Wilmington	1941	St. Louis (NL)	1	—
Sam McConnell	Philadelphia	1915	Philadelphia (AL)	6	.182

Name	Birthplace	Years Played	Teams	G	W	L
Jim McGarr	Philadelphia	1912	Detroit	1		.000
Pat Meaney	Philadelphia	1912	Detroit	1		.000
Bill Mellor	Camden	1902	Baltimore	10		.361
Ferdy Moore	Camden	1914	Philadelphia (AL)	2		.500
Jesse Purnell	Glenside	1904	Philadelphia (NL)	7		.105
Ben Rochefort	Camden	1914	Philadelphia (AL)	1		.500
George Stutz	Philadelphia	1926	Philadelphia (NL)	6		.000
Allie Watt	Philadelphia	1920	Washington	1		1.000

OUTFIELDERS

Name	Birthplace	Years Played	Teams	G	BA
Charlie Bates	Philadelphia	1927	Philadelphia (AL)	9	.237
John Castle	Honey Brook	1910	Philadelphia (NL)	3	.250
Tod Dennehey	Philadelphia	1923	Philadelphia (NL)	9	.292
George Durning	Philadelphia	1925	Philadelphia (NL)	5	.357
Chick Hartley	Philadelphia	1902	New York (NL)	1	.000
John Jones	Coatesville	1923, 1932	Philadelphia (AL)	5	.200
Dan Kerwin	Philadelphia	1903	Cincinnati	2	.667
Tom Kirk	Philadelphia	1947	Philadelphia (AL)	1	.000
Bill Leinhauser	Philadelphia	1912	Detroit	1	.000
Bob Lindemann	Philadelphia	1901	Philadelphia (AL)	3	.111
Tommy Madden	Philadelphia	1906, 1910	Boston (NL), New York (AL)	5	.250
Billy Maharg	Philadelphia	1912, 1916	Detroit, Philadelphia (NL)	2	.000
Red McDermott	Philadelphia	1912	Detroit	5	.267
Dan McGarvey	Philadelphia	1912	Detroit	1	.000
Joe O'Rourke	Philadelphia	1929	Philadelphia (NL)	3	.000
Mike Pasquella	Philadelphia	1919	Philadelphia, St. Louis (both NL)	2	.500
Ty Pickup	Philadelphia	1918	Philadelphia (NL)	1	1.000
Bill Thomas	Norristown	1902	Philadelphia (NL)	6	.118
Ham Wade	Spring City	1907	New York (NL)	1	—
Ed Watkins	Philadelphia	1902	Philadelphia (NL)	1	.000

OTHERS (NO POSITION PLAYED)

Name	Birthplace	Years Played	Teams	G	BA
Joe Green	Philadelphia	1924	Philadelphia (AL)	1	.000
Tom Maher	Philadelphia	1902	Philadelphia (NL)	1	—
Gene Patton	Coatesville	1944	Boston (NL)	1	—
Rob Sasser	Philadelphia	1998	Texas	1	.000
Bert Yeabsley	Philadelphia	1919	Philadelphia (NL)	3	—

MANAGERS

Name	Birthplace	Years	Teams	Record	Pct.
Lena Blackburne	Clifton Heights	1928–29	Chicago (AL)	99–133	.427
Harry Davis	Philadelphia	1912	Cleveland	54–71	.432
Jimmy Dykes	Philadelphia	1934–46, 1951–54, 1958–61	Chicago, Philadelphia (both AL), Baltimore, Cincinnati, Detroit, Cleveland	1,406–1,541	.477
Lee Elia	Philadelphia	1982–83, 1987–88	Chicago, Philadelphia (both NL)	238–300	.442
Kid Gleason	Camden	1919–1923	Chicago (AL)	392–364	.519
Dallas Green	Newport, NJ	1979–81, 1989, 1993–96	Philadelphia (NL), New York (AL & NL)	454–478	.487
Joe Kerrigan	Philadelphia	2001	Boston	17–26	.395
Tom Lasorda	Norristown	1976–96	Los Angeles	1,599–1,439	.526
Hans Lobert	Wilmington	1938, 1942	Philadelphia (NL)	42–111	.275
Joe McCarthy	Philadelphia	1926–46, 1948–50	Chicago (NL), New York (AL), Boston (AL)	2,125–1,333	.615
Danny Murtaugh	Chester	1957–64, 1967, 1970–71, 1973–76	Pittsburgh	1,115–950	.540
Mike Scioscia	Upper Darby	2000–02	Anaheim	256–230	.527
Bill Shettsline	Philadelphia	1898–1902	Philadelphia (NL)	367–303	.548
Eddie Stanky	Philadelphia	1952–55, 1966–68, 1977	St. Louis (NL), Chicago (AL), Texas	467–435	.518

Name	Birthplace	Years	Teams	Record	Pct.
Mickey Vernon	Marcus Hook	1961–63	Washington	135–227	.373
Bucky Walters	Philadelphia	1948–49	Cincinnati	81–123	.397
Jimmie Wilson	Philadelphia	1934–38, 1941–44	Philadelphia, Chicago (both NL)	493–735	.401

Photo Credits

New York Yankees: Pages 7, 81, 91

National Baseball Hall of Fame Library, Cooperstown, NY:
Pages 10, 17, 19, 22, 24, 29, 32, 39, 42, 43, 46, 50, 55, 57, 62,
64, 65, 67, 84, 86, 89, 97, 110, 112, 114, 115, 117, 118

Philadelphia Phillies: Pages 13, 46, 93, 94, 104, 105, 107

Delaware County *Daily Times:* Pages 15, 53, 101

Rich Westcott: Pages 26, 35, 41, 45, 47, 58, 95

Philadelphia Athletics Historical Society: Pages 37, 94

Texas Rangers: Page 51

Cincinnati Reds: Page 52

Kansas City Royals: Page 62

Seattle Mariners: Pages 68, 75

Atlanta Braves: Page 69

New York Mets: Pages 73, 76

Detroit Tigers: Page 75

Arizona Diamondbacks: Page 78

Boston Red Sox: Page 79
San Francisco Giants: Page 79
St. Louis Cardinals: Pages 82, 90
Los Angeles Dodgers: Page 99
Anaheim Angels: Page 102

About the Author

Rich Westcott is a lifelong resident of the Philadelphia area who has known or covered many of the players in this book. His own baseball career came to an inglorious conclusion when he flunked a trial with the Philadelphia Athletics (remember them?). Westcott has been a newspaper and magazine writer and editor for more than 40 years, and is the founder and former editor and publisher of *Phillies Report.* He is the author of 13 other books, including 12 on baseball.